HARVESTING THE FRUITS

HARVESTING THE FRUITS

Aspects of Christian Faith in Ecumenical Dialogue

Cardinal Walter Kasper

continuum

Published by the Continuum International Publishing Group

The Tower Building   80 Maiden Lane
11 York Road   Suite 704
London   New York
SE1 7NX   NY 10038

www.continuumbooks.com

First published 2009

British Library Cataloguing-in-Publication Data
A catalogue record for this book is available from the British Library.

ISBN 978-1441-16272-4

Designed and typeset by BookEns, Royston, Herts.
Printed and bound by the MPG Books Group

Ecumenical Consensus, Convergences and Differences

Lutheran–Catholic dialogue (1967–present)

Reformed–Catholic dialogue (1970–present)

Anglican–Catholic dialogue (1970–present)

Methodist–Catholic dialogue (1967–present)

*"For we will reap at harvest time,
if we do not give up"*

(Gal 6:9)

Table of Contents

List of Abbreviations

Phase IV (1995–2006)
L–C *Apostolicity* = *The Apostolicity of the Church (2006)*

INTERNATIONAL DIALOGUE BETWEEN THE CATHOLIC CHURCH AND THE WORLD ALLIANCE OF REFORMED CHURCHES

Phase I (1970–1977)
Ref I = *The Presence of Christ in Church and World (1977)*

Phase II (1984–1990)
Ref II = *Towards a Common Understanding of the Church (1990)*

Phase III (1998–2005)
Ref III = *The Church as Community of Common Witness to the Kingdom of God (2007)*

INTERNATIONAL DIALOGUE BETWEEN THE ANGLICAN COMMUNION AND THE ROMAN CATHOLIC CHURCH

Preparatory Commission (1967-68)
ARCIC *Malta* = *Malta Report of the Preparatory Commission (1968)*

ARCIC I (1970–1981)
ARCIC *Eucharist* = *Eucharistic Doctrine (1971)*
ARCIC *Ministry* = *Ministry and Ordination (1973)*
ARCIC *Authority I* = *Authority in the Church I (1976)*
ARCIC *Eucharist Elucidation* = *Eucharistic Doctrine: Elucidation (1979)*
ARCIC *Ministry Elucidation* = *Ministry and Ordination: Elucidation (1979)*

ARCIC *Authority I Elucidation*	=	*Authority in the Church I: Elucidation (1981)*
ARCIC *Authority II*	=	*Authority in the Church II (1981)*
ARCIC *FR Preface*	=	*Preface to the 'Final Report' (1982)*
ARCIC *FR Introduction*	=	*Introduction to the 'Final Report' (1982)*
ARCIC *FR Conclusion*	=	*Conclusion to the 'Final Report' (1982)*
ARCIC *Clarifications*	=	*Clarifications of Certain Aspects of the Agreed Statements on Eucharist and Ministry (1994)* (endorsed by ARCIC II)

ARCIC II (1983–2005)

ARCIC *Salvation*	=	*Salvation and the Church (1987)*
ARCIC *Church*	=	*Church as Communion (1991)*
ARCIC *Life in Christ*	=	*Life in Christ: Morals, Communion and the Church (1994)*
ARCIC *Gift*	=	*The Gift of Authority: Authority in the Church III (1999)*
ARCIC *Mary*	=	*Mary: Grace and Hope in Christ (2005)*

International Anglican–Roman Catholic Commission for Unity and Mission (IARCCUM)

IARCCUM *GTUM*	=	*Growing Together in Unity and Mission (2007)*

International Commission for Dialogue between the Roman Catholic Church and the World Methodist Council

M–C *Denver*	=	*The Denver Report (1971)*
M–C *Dublin*	=	*The Dublin Report (1976)*

M–C *Honolulu*	=	*Toward an Agreed Statement on the Holy Spirit (1981)*
M–C *Nairobi*	=	*Towards a Statement on the Church (1986)*
M–C *Singapore*	=	*The Apostolic Tradition (1991)*
M–C *Rio*	=	*The Word of Life (1996)*
M–C *Brighton*	=	*Speaking the Truth in Love (2001)*
M–C *Seoul*	=	*The Grace Given You in Christ (2006)*

COMMONLY USED ABBREVIATIONS

AAS	*Acta Apostolicae Sedis*
Apol.	Apology of the Augsburg Confession
ARCIC	Anglican – Roman Catholic International Commission
BC	Book of Concord
BEM	*Baptism, Eucharist and Ministry*
CA	Confessio Augustana (Augsburg Confession)
DV	*Dei verbum,* Second Vatican Council, Dogmatic Constitution on Divine Revelation
GTUM	*Growing Together in Unity and Mission*
IARCCUM	International Anglican–Roman Catholic Commission for Unity and Mission
JDDJ	*Joint Declaration on the Doctrine of Justification*
JWG	Joint Working Group (between the World Council of Churches and the Roman Catholic Church)
L–C	Lutheran–Catholic (when referring to the documents of the International Lutheran–Roman Catholic Commission on Unity)
LG	*Lumen gentium,* Second Vatican Council, Dogmatic Constitution on the Church
LWF	Lutheran World Federation

M–C	Methodist–Catholic (when referring to the documents of the International Commission for Dialogue between the Roman Catholic Church and the World Methodist Council)
Ref I, II, III	Reformed–Catholic Church (when referring to the documents of the International Dialogue between the Catholic Church and the World Alliance of Reformed Churches
UR	*Unitatis redintegratio,* Second Vatican Council, Decree on Ecumenism
UUS	*Ut unum sint,* John Paul II, Encyclical on Commitment to Ecumenism
VELKD	Vereinigte Evangelisch–Lutherische Kirche Deutschlands (United Evangelical Lutheran Church of Germany)
WA	The complete writings of Luther are found in the 'Weimar edition'
WARC	World Alliance of Reformed Churches
WCC	World Council of Churches
WMC	World Methodist Council

Introduction

1. The Second Vatican Council in its Decree on Ecumenism *Unitatis redintegratio* (1964) *(UR)* declared the restoration of unity among all Christians to be one of its principal concerns. The Council recalled that "Christ the Lord founded one Church and one Church only". Accordingly, division among Christians "openly contradicts the will of Christ, scandalises the world, and damages that most holy cause, the preaching of the Gospel to every creature" (*UR* 1).

    With this Decree the Second Vatican Council formally brought the Catholic Church into the ecumenical movement, and set in motion a series of ecumenical dialogues on the international level, but also on the regional and local levels. Since then there have been more than four decades of official international bilateral ecumenical dialogues between the Catholic Church and the Christian world communions. These dialogues have produced an impressive number of ecumenical documents, which give witness to the common search to fulfil the will of our one Lord Jesus Christ "that all may be one" (John 17:21). In keeping with this prayer the dialogues have aimed at overcoming the painful differences and separations of the past, and, on the basis of our common faith in Jesus Christ, have sought to pave the way for full visible communion in truth and love.

With gratitude to the Lord and his guiding Spirit, and to all who have contributed to this ecumenical pilgrimage, we can affirm that many prejudices and misunderstandings of the past have been overcome, that bridges of new mutual understanding and practical cooperation have been built. In many cases convergences and consensus have been found, and old – although unfortunately still existing – differences have been better identified.

Nevertheless, in many respects the ecumenical scene today is changing rapidly. The original enthusiasm has given way to a new sobriety; questions about the ecumenical methods and the achievements of the past decades, and doubts about the future, are being expressed. A new generation of ecumenically minded and motivated Christians, especially among the laity, is taking up the torch of the ecumenical movement, but with a different emphasis with respect to its predecessors.

In order not to forget the constructive outcome of the last decades – nor to overlook what still remains to be done – it was necessary to undertake a fresh and unprecedented effort to *harvest* the rich results of some of the dialogues with the Western partners and identify the remaining tasks. We embark on this project *in via* looking back in grateful fidelity to what has been achieved, and to the future with the desire to provide responsible and encouraging guidance. With this in mind we hope to initiate and to facilitate the reception of dialogue results in the Catholic Church and with four partners from whom we are still divided, and to foster further dialogue regarding questions that are still open.

Most of our dialogues have resulted in study documents of Joint Commissions appointed by the churches involved,[1] but they are not binding authoritative texts. Therefore they need reception and recognition in the Church and by the Church.[2] This study document intends to initiate, to promote and to facilitate forms of reception of dialogue results in our Church and in our divided partner church communities as well. Awareness of the degree of apostolic faith that we already share can then foster further dialogues on still open questions and inspire new enthusiasm and a greater degree of common witness in today's world.

It is therefore timely to ask: Where are we? What has been achieved? What has still to be done? Where *can* we, and where *should* we, move ahead?

2.   Though the Pontifical Council has undertaken dialogues both with the Eastern Churches and with the ecclesial communities originating in the West, we focus in this document on the reports of the Western bilateral international dialogues[3] with our first dialogue partners after the Second Vatican Council, namely: the Lutheran World Federation (LWF), the World Methodist Council (WMC), the Anglican Communion, and the World Alliance of Reformed Churches (WARC). The Lutheran and the Reformed churches identify directly with the magisterial Reformation of the sixteenth century, whereas the Anglican Communion occupies a special place among the communions influenced by the Reformation movement. Methodism grew out of the Anglican tradition in the eighteenth century, but many of the differences which separate Methodists and Catholics today date from the Reformation period. Furthermore, in associating its member churches with the *Joint Declaration on the Doctrine of Justification (JDDJ)* signed by the LWF and the Catholic Church, the WMC aligned itself to a major initiative in resolving a key area of conflict inherited from the sixteenth century. Other dialogue partners from the Free Churches,

and Evangelical, Charismatic and Pentecostal traditions, which are not dealt with in this context, would require a different consideration.

Whereas each of the four dialogues mentioned above was bilateral, and though there is a commitment to continue each of these bilateral dialogues, the objective of this document is to reflect on the results of these four bilateral dialogues together, and their interrelationships with one another. The task of bringing bilateral dialogues into a larger multilateral context carries with it some risks and challenges, since each dialogue has its own origin, logic and methodology, and its own dynamic and character. As a result, the intention and focus of each bilateral dialogue is different from the others. Even when considering the same issues, their difference of focus often means that they treat them from different perspectives, and come to a different degree of consensus or convergence. The present project, therefore, tries as much as possible to maintain the distinct character of the four dialogues.

At the same time, however, there is a growing interrelatedness of our dialogue partners, resulting from the concords and agreements made among themselves. Frequently, these have softened old confessional boundaries, profiles and differences, for example: the Leuenberg Concord (1973), Meissen Declaration (1988), Porvoo Common Statement (1992), Waterloo Declaration (2001), Reuilly Common Statement (2001), the Report of the Joint Working Group between the LWF and the WARC *Called to Communion and Common Witness* (2002) and others, and the more recent united and uniting churches on national levels. Indeed, by examining central themes of Christian faith and ecumenical dialogues, it has been possible to discern many points of consensus or convergence – and indeed remaining questions and differences – *across* the four dialogues. Moreover, today all churches face the same or similar challenges. Thus a differentiated common treatment of the four dialogues seems to be possible and appropriate as well.

3.   The current project is grounded in the Catholic understanding of ecumenical dialogue and the principles on ecumenism as stated by the Second Vatican Council (*Lumen gentium [LG]* 8 and 15; *UR* 2–4) and subsequent magisterial documents, most notably the encyclical of Pope John Paul II *Ut unum sint* (1995) *[UUS]*. The Council sees in the ecumenical movement an impulse of the Holy Spirit at work, who awakened in divided Christians remorse over their divisions and has bestowed upon them longing for unity (*UR* 1; 4); He has initiated the pilgrimage towards unity, which is not possible without conversion, renewal and reform (*UR* 6–8; *UUS* 15).[4]

As a result, today our discussions no longer take as their starting point the differences between us, but what we have in common – above all our common confession of the Triune God and of Jesus as Lord and Saviour (used as the basic formula of the WCC, and cited in *UR* 1). Accordingly, this present document takes as its starting point the acknowledgment that through common Baptism a real but incomplete communion exists between the Catholic Church and the dialogue partners identified above, a degree of communion which varies from one bilateral relation to another (*UR* 3).

On the basis and in the context of what we have in common, we try to understand better what divides us, and to engage in a dialogue regarding the issues involved. Such a dialogue in truth and in love is not only an exchange of *ideas*, but an exchange of *gifts* (*UUS* 28), which can always enrich and challenge both partners. Dialogue presupposes partners who have, and who are aware of, a strong sense of the identity of their respective churches. Accordingly, ecumenical dialogue has nothing to do with relativism and indifferentism towards the doctrine of the faith. Its goal is not syncretism or unity on the lowest common denominator or peaceful coexistence in division, but full visible communion in faith, sacramental life, apostolic ministry and mission. Full communion does not mean uniformity, but exists alongside cultural diversity, different liturgical rites, different forms of piety, different but complementary emphases and perspectives, etc. In this sense "ecumenism is directed precisely to making the partial communion existing between Christians grow toward full communion in truth and charity" (*UUS* 14).[5]

In the end, Jesus Christ himself is the basis and the goal of all our dialogue. Through our common Baptism we are in Him, and to the degree we are fully united with Him we will be united also among ourselves in a unity according to the exemplar and source of the mystery of unity in the Holy Trinity (cf. *UR* 2).

In order to reach this ultimate goal, ecumenical dialogue seeks step by step to achieve many intermediate goals. It could be said that the ecumenical movement is a common pilgrimage, by means of different forms of dialogue, which intimately belong together and complement each other. Thus ecumenical dialogue is theological dialogue in truth and practical cooperation, a dialogue of love and life; at its heart it is a spiritual dialogue.[6]

One major difficulty in all these dialogues is that there is not a complete symmetry or level relationship between the Catholic Church and the above-mentioned ecumenical partners. Whereas, on the Catholic side, the living Magisterium provides a basis and reference point, for our partners such a teaching office does not exist in the same way. Yet although their sources and points of reference are not as firm and as authoritatively binding as on the Catholic side, our partners do not merely express personal positions, but also refer to their confessional writings, or to other more or less recognised authorities (eg, Luther and Calvin, writings and hymns of Wesley, Anglican liturgy, more recent official statements, etc.). As common ground we have the Holy Scriptures and the witness of the Church Fathers.

4. For this project we have chosen four main issues of the above mentioned dialogues: Jesus Christ and the Holy Trinity; Salvation, Justification, Sanctification; The Church; The Sacraments of Baptism and Eucharist. These, we believe, are the principal issues of the dialogues. At the same time, we are aware that there are also other important issues treated in individual dialogues, but not by the others, and therefore these are not represented here (for instance the place of Mary in Christian doctrine and life, as treated in the ARCIC dialogue and in some regional dialogues).

Each of the four chapters begins with a short description of the often polemical controversies in the Reformation period and the following centuries. Next, the body of the chapter describes and analyses the progress which has been made through the dialogues leading to many convergences and some consensus, but also exposing open questions and remaining differences. Each chapter concludes with a reflection and evaluation section. The final chapter contains *Preliminary Conclusions*, which attempt to summarise the positive achievements and remaining questions, and look objectively towards the future.

Looking back on what has been achieved in more than forty years, we have every reason to be grateful to the Lord for the rich fruits that we have harvested from our dialogues. There is no reason to be discouraged or frustrated, or to speak of an 'ecumenical winter'. The Spirit who initiated the ecumenical movement has also accompanied it and made it fruitful. We have achieved more then we could have imagined or dreamed forty years ago. Yet we must also admit, realistically, that we have not yet reached the goal of our ecumenical pilgrimage, but are still at an intermediate stage. There remain fundamental problems to solve and differences to overcome, which we believe we have identified more clearly here. This document will enable us to move forward with a clearer sense of direction, and with new courage and hope.

Many interested, skilful, diligent and ecumenically committed people have contributed to the realisation of this document. First among these must be mentioned former and present Staff members and Consultors of the Pontifical Council for Promoting Christian Unity, who collected and synthesised the rich material, and whose advice greatly helped in its evaluation. A first draft was presented to the Plenary Assembly of the PCPCU in December 2008. The overall reaction was positive, while the many critical remarks and positive proposals led to a thorough reworking of the whole text. The first draft was also sent to some theologians in our partner churches. We are also grateful for their reactions, both positive and critical, which were of considerable help in the final re-editing undertaken by the PCPCU in close cooperation with the Consultors and experts of this Council.

We hope that this study document may prove a stimulus for our Church and for our partners, to reflect on the common path and dialogue process of over forty years, to keep it alive, evaluate it and then continue the dialogues with fresh insights and new courage. Then, we may together take those further steps which, with God's help, will lead us some day to full communion, expressed in sharing at the one table of the Lord.

NOTES

1 For reasons of simplicity and brevity in what follows the term 'church' is sometimes also used for Protestant communities according to their own self–designation and self–understanding (e.g., WCC – World Council of Churches, Church of England, EKD – Evangelical Church of Germany, etc.). The theological difference in the Catholic and Protestant uses of this term is clearly indicated in Chapter Three.

2 The Catholic Church has given a certain degree of recognition to ARCIC I on Eucharist and ministry and has formally signed the Lutheran–Catholic *Joint Declaration on the Doctrine of Justification*.

3 The multilateral dialogues and the many national dialogue documents, which often prepared the way for international dialogues, or deepened and completed them, could not be considered in explicit detail. The most important ones are mentioned in the footnotes so that they can be easily compared with the international bilateral results.

4 On this issue cf. the document of the Groupe des Dombes: *Pour la conversion des Églises* (1991).

5 Other models of unity differing from the Catholic understanding of the goal of ecumenism, as stated here, can be found in the Lutheran–Roman Catholic dialogue document *Facing Unity – Models, Forms and Phases of Catholic–Lutheran Church Fellowship* (1984).

6 Practical suggestions can be found in the *Directory for the Application of Principles and Norms on Ecumenism* (1993) and in Cardinal Kasper's *A Handbook of Spiritual Ecumenism* (2007).

Chapter One

Fundamentals of our Common Faith: Jesus Christ and the Holy Trinity

INTRODUCTION

5. The Reformers of the sixteenth century did not intend to create a new Church, but sought rather to remain in the Tradition of the one, holy, catholic and apostolic Church through the ages. They officially endorsed the creedal statements of the ancient Church, and accepted the Trinitarian and the Christological confessions as expressed in these creedal statements.[7] Thus the Trinitarian and Christological confession of the Bible and the ancient Church remained as common basis in spite of all other divisions.

But the disputes during the Reformation period gave rise on each side to serious doubts whether the Gospel of Jesus Christ was properly understood by their opponents, and given its rightful place at the centre of Christian proclamation and life. The Protestant Reformers, for example, argued that the theology and praxis of indulgences contradicted the fundamental belief that we have been justified by God's grace, and they felt therefore that the Gospel was being distorted. Polemics proliferated especially over the questions of justification, the sacrificial character of the mass, and the papacy. Catholics saw in the rejection of these doctrines a rejection of apostolic faith handed down by the Tradition of the Church through the ages. In such an atmosphere, the apostolic heritage shared by all was frequently overshadowed, overlooked and forgotten.

6. In the ecumenical movement the common Trinitarian and Christological heritage became fundamental for seeking reconciliation among divided Christian communities. It had been developing through the establishment and self-understanding of the World Council of Churches (WCC), and subsequently through the achievements of the Second Vatican Council. The 1948 Assembly of the WCC spoke of itself as "a fellowship which seeks to express that unity in Christ already given to us and to prepare the way for a much fuller and much deeper expression of that unity". This statement was deepened by the New Delhi formulation of 1961, which spoke of "a fellowship of churches which confess the Lord Jesus Christ as God and Saviour according to the scriptures, and therefore seek to fulfil together their common calling to the glory of the one God, Father, Son and Holy Spirit."

The Second Vatican Council's Decree on Ecumenism spoke of the movement towards the restoration of unity among all Christians as being "fostered by the grace of the Holy Spirit", and echoed affirmingly the New Delhi text in stating: "Taking part in this movement, which is called ecumenical, are those who invoke the Triune God and confess Jesus as Lord and Saviour" (UR 1). It is significant that the Apostles' and Nicene-Constantinopolitan Creeds, which have been used in the Week of Prayer materials prepared annually by the Catholic Church and the Faith and Order Commission of the WCC over the past 40 years, are understood as commonly held expressions of Christian faith.[8]

The four dialogues treated in this study have addressed the Trinitarian and Christological foundations of faith and the early creeds in the context of developing and setting forth a theological framework within which to address other points of difference. The dialogues demonstrate a high level of agreement on these basic issues, which is essential as we aim at restoring unity among Christians.

A. THE GOSPEL OF JESUS CHRIST

7. The Gospel of Jesus Christ, preached by the apostles, is the source of all saving truth and the basis of all ecumenical dialogue.

The Lutheran-Catholic dialogue affirms agreement on the gospel by stating, "What God has done for the salvation of the world in Jesus Christ is transmitted in the gospel and made present in the Holy Spirit. The gospel as proclamation of God's saving action is therefore itself a saving event. . . . Out of and in the service of the proclamation of the gospel, certain writings were composed which were later designated as the New Testament" (L–C *Malta*, 16-17). Shortly afterwards: "Lutherans and Catholics alike are convinced that the gospel is the foundation of Christian freedom" (L–C *Malta*, 30). "As affirmed in the *Joint Declaration on the Doctrine of Justification*, by our common faith in the gospel we hold to the heart of the New Testament witness to God's saving action in Christ" (L–C *Apostolicity*, 432; cf. *JDDJ*, 17).

The Reformed–Catholic dialogue begins its treatment of Christ's relationship to the Church with a reference to the Gospel's central content and a statement on the shared task that the gospel imposes. "The starting point of these discussions was the recognition that, in Jesus Christ, God has made joint cause with sinful humanity and aims at the renewal of the world. Therefore all those who are connected with the name of Jesus Christ have the joint task of bearing witness to this Gospel" (*Ref I*, 13). The same text describes the church-founding impact of the gospel: "Christ sends us into the world with the message of new life and a new common life in fellowship with him. In our speaking and acting he bears witness to himself. His Gospel gathers, protects and maintains the *koinonia* of his disciples as a sign and beginning of his kingdom" (*Ref I*, 75). This dialogue speaks of the gospel among the shared concerns basic to the Lutheran and Reformed churches, namely, "to hear and proclaim the message of the gospel as the one word of God which alone brings authentic faith into being" (*Ref II*, 18; cf. 68). Regarding Jesus crucified and raised: "This is the news, still surprising and overwhelming, which constitutes the gospel; of this the church is the beneficiary and herald" (*Ref II*, 70).

The Anglican–Catholic dialogue describes the gospel as "the good news of salvation," while linking it to faith in Jesus, to the earliest Christian preaching and to the New Testament. "Through the gift of the Spirit the apostolic community came to recognize in the words and deeds of Jesus the saving activity of God and their mission to proclaim to all men the good news of salvation. Therefore they preached Jesus through whom God has spoken finally to men. Assisted by the Holy Spirit they transmitted what they had heard and seen of the life and words of Jesus and their interpretation of his redemptive work. Consequently the inspired documents in which this is related came to be accepted by the Church as a normative record of the authentic foundation of the faith" (ARCIC *Authority I*, 2).

The Methodist-Catholic dialogue states, "God has spoken definitively to us in the Son, so much so that he is called God's Word, the Word made flesh (John 1:1-18). ... When the apostles preached Christ, they proclaimed Christ crucified and risen.... The person of Christ, his teaching and work for us: it was to all this that the apostles bore witness, for all this is God's Word. ... As the gospel was preached by the apostles, the church was called together" (M–C *Singapore*, 9-12; cf. M–C *Rio*, 17-18). In the ongoing life of the Church the gospel sounds forth, for "[w]hen there is faithful witness to Jesus Christ, people hear through the words of witness the word of God and know through deeds of love the God of love. To such witness in word and deed all the faithful are called ..." (M–C *Rio*, 23).

Christians have had various understandings of the transmission of the Gospel of Jesus Christ, and this is taken up in Chapter Three.

B.   THE CREEDS

8.   Dialogue reports show the importance of the creeds for separated Christians seeking to underline a commonly shared apostolic faith, either presenting the Nicene Creed or the Apostles' Creed in full (e.g., M-C *Singapore*, 38, and IARCCUM *GTUM*, 11, respectively), or giving common testimony that the central aspects of faith are expressed in the creeds. Lutherans and Catholics affirm together, "The starting point is the common affirmation of the faith of the early church, formulated by the early councils in obedience to holy scripture and witnessed to in the creeds of the early church (Apostles' Creed, Nicene Creed, Athanasian Creed)" (L–C *Facing Unity,* 57).

ARCIC affirms that "[i]n both our traditions the appeal to Scripture, to the creeds, to the Fathers and to the definitions of the councils of the early Church is regarded as basic and normative" (ARCIC *Authority I*, 18).

The Methodist–Catholic dialogue states, "The Christian Church professes the Apostles' and the Nicene–Constantinopolitan Creeds, which are Christological and Trinitarian. They name the Father, the Son, and the Holy Spirit, and they place the life, death and resurrection of the Word incarnate at the centre of the articles of faith. The creeds embody the biblical teaching about God and Christ. Their confession is incorporated in the Church's liturgies . . . and also function as a rule of faith *(regula fidei)*, normative for conciliar and other official teaching" (M–C *Brighton*, 11; cf. *Rio,* 34–35)

In some dialogues, in illustrating common ground on liturgy, partners bear witness to the importance of the creeds *as a shared aspect of worship.* Reformed and Catholics testify that "[a] common profession of faith, such as the Nicene Creed, reminds us of our belonging to the church of all times and of all places, now manifest in our own community" (*Ref III*, 166). Anglicans and Catholics affirm that "[i]n liturgical celebrations, we regularly make the same trinitarian profession of faith in the form of the Apostles' Creed or the Nicene–Constantinopolitan Creed" (IARCCUM *GTUM*, 13; cf. Common Declaration Paul VI–Archbishop Coggan, 1977, 2). Methodists and Catholics state that "[t]he Nicene Creed, used by both Catholics and Methodists in their liturgy and teaching, is a comprehensive and authoritative statement of Christian faith. . ." (M–C *Singapore*, 38; cf. *Rio*, 112).

The reports, in referring to the *Creeds in the life of the Church*, also single out the creedal marks of the Church, namely that it is *one, holy, catholic and apostolic*. The Reformed–Catholic dialogue acknowledged succinctly that "ecclesiological insights can be gathered from [the Church fathers' writings concerning] the nature, mission and structure of the church, and might be gathered together under the four headings appearing as its marks in the Creed: one, holy, catholic and apostolic" (*Ref III*, 49). ARCIC states that "[t]he Church points to its source and mission when it confesses in the Creed, 'We believe in one holy catholic and apostolic Church' " (ARCIC *Church*, 25). Methodists and Catholics "joyfully affirm together in the Nicene–Constantinopolitan Creed 'one, holy, catholic and apostolic Church'. These four traditional 'marks' or 'notes' of the Church derive from its creation by and its communion with the Triune God" (M–C *Seoul*, 65).

In summary, the Nicene–Constantinopolitan Creed and the Apostles' Creed are seen, in this ecumenical context, as essential expressions which formulate the significant degree of the one apostolic faith which Christians share, and have always shared, despite their divisions.

C. THE HOLY TRINITY

1. *The Holy Trinity as Principle of Communion*

9. The dialogues generally take the Trinitarian foundations of Christian faith as a given, but nonetheless offer a consistent witness to the richness of that shared Trinitarian faith.

The Lutheran–Catholic dialogue declares, "Together we confess the faith in the Triune God and the saving work of God through Jesus Christ in the Holy Spirit, which binds all

Christendom together (*Confessio Augustana* [CA] I and III). Through all the disputes and differences of the sixteenth century, Lutheran and Catholic Christians remained one in this central and most important truth of the Christian faith" (L–C *Christ,* 13). This profession of faith in the Trinity is possible because of our encounter with the life and teaching, death and resurrection of Christ, and because of the sending of the Holy Spirit at Pentecost. The Reformed–Catholic dialogue states, "The work of Jesus, the Son, reveals to us the role of the Spirit of God who is common to him and to the Father: it reveals . . . that God is triune" (*Ref II*, 74). Similarly, the Methodist–Catholic dialogue states, "It is primarily through the missions of the Son in the Incarnation and of the Spirit after the resurrection in the foundation and life of the Church that we come to know that the one God is Trinity and are led into some understanding of the work of the three Persons through God's saving acts in history" (M–C *Honolulu*, 11; cf. *Rio,* 108).

The documents ponder the inner life of the Trinity. "The mystery of the divine life cannot be captured by human thought and language, but in speaking of God as Trinity in Unity, Father, Son and Holy Spirit, we are affirming that the Being of God is a unity of self–communicating and interdependent relationships" (ARCIC *Life in Christ*, 7; cf. IARCCUM *GTUM,* 14). The Methodist–Catholic dialogue speaks of "the invisible *koinonia* that is the life of the Holy Trinity", and elsewhere, of "the exchange of love that is the life of the blessed Trinity, Father, Son and Holy Spirit" (M–C *Seoul*, 60 and *Singapore*, 53; cf. ARCIC *Church*, 15). The inner life of the Trinity – "the life of God, Father, Son and Holy Spirit" – is indeed "the life God wills to share with all people" (ARCIC *Church*, 3). The Triune God is the author of life in all its fullness (ARCIC *Gift*, 7). He "is one in the communion of three Persons; perfect in holy love; comprehensive in his reconciling purpose; and utterly generous in the sending of the Son and the Holy Spirit" (M–C *Seoul*, 65, citing *Called to Love and Praise*, 2.4).

The Trinity calls the Church into being for the redemption of humankind; each of the dialogues reflects on this mystery in related ways. The Lutheran–Catholic dialogue notes, "According to the witness of the New Testament, our salvation, the justification of sinners and the existence of the church are indissolubly linked with the triune God and are founded in him alone" (L–C *Church and Justification*, 6). The mystery of the Trinity determines and permeates Jesus' whole work (cf. L–C *Church and Justification*, 12), and the unity he desires for his disciples is a unity "created in the image and likeness of the Triune God" (L–C *Ways, 44). The Reformed–Catholic dialogue speaks of the movement in which the eternal Father, "for Christ's sake and through him, accepts and recreates the lost world in the Holy Spirit" (Ref I,* 81). ARCIC notes, "The will of God, Father, Son and Holy Spirit, is to reconcile to himself all that he has created and sustains, to set free the creation from its bondage to decay, and to draw all humanity into communion with himself" (ARCIC *Salvation*, 1). "The biblical witness has led the Church to the conviction that Father and Son and Spirit were giving themselves for the redemption of us all" (M–C *Rio*, 25; cf. ARCIC *Church*, 16; *Life in Christ*, 4). The Methodist–Catholic dialogue speaks at length of the mystery of the Holy Trinity being at the heart of the mystery of the Church and at the foundation of its mission. "The Church springs from an initiative by the Holy Trinity" (M–C *Seoul*, 52); its "deepest and hidden reality, the mystery that lies at the heart of its nature and mission", is "the invisible presence of the Triune God, the one God who is Father, Son and Holy Spirit, the God who is Holy Love" (M–C *Seoul*, 49).

"Communion with the Triune God is the very life of the Church; communion with the mission of God's Son and Spirit is the very mission of the Church" (M–C *Seoul*, 74; cf. 51; cf. also *Rio*, 73; *Singapore*, 9; L–C *Church and Justification*, 5, 48).

2. The Holy Trinity in Salvation History

a) The Father: source of salvation history

10. The Lutheran-Catholic dialogue states, "Like every good gift, unity also comes from the Father through the Son in the Holy Spirit. The will and work of the Father is 'in Christ as a plan for the fullness of time, to unite all things in him' (Eph 1:10). In the Father is the origin of all the Son does for unity" (L–C *Ways*, 9). Testimony is given that "[t]he Father is the absolutely primary principle for he is 'source, guide and goal of all that is' (Rom 11:36; cf. 1 Cor 8:6)" (*Ref I*, 46). "God is present in the world as its Creator, Sustainer, Lord of history who rules all things as Loving Father" (*Ref I*, 43). "The Creator of the world ... through the revelation of his will ... leads mankind onto the road of salvation and in Jesus Christ offers it the gift of final redemption ... and participation in His divine life and thus in His freedom" (*Ref I*, 51). "To bring us to union with himself, the Father sent into the world Jesus Christ, his only Son, in whom all things were created" (ARCIC *Salvation*, 1). "The Father's overflowing love created humanity for communion with himself, and that same creative love gathers together the followers of his Son into the visible community of the Church.... By the unitive power of his Spirit of love, the Father draws us into a communion of life with his own beloved Son... All of this is the fruit of the outpouring of the Father's creative and gathering love" (M–C *Seoul*, 54; cf. *Rio*, 73, 108; *Singapore*, 7).

Reports testify to our jointly held belief that the Father is the source of the procession of the other persons of the Trinity.[9] According to the *Joint Declaration on the Doctrine of Justification*, "The Father sent his Son into the world to save sinners. The foundation and presupposition of justification is the incarnation, death and resurrection of Christ. Justification thus means that Christ himself is our righteousness, in which we share through the Holy Spirit in accord with the will of the Father" (L–C *JDDJ*, 15). Furthermore, "Christ who is Lord of all and active in creation points to God the Father who, in the Spirit, leads and guides history" (*Ref I*, 45). ARCIC states that "Jesus spoke and acted with authority because of his perfect communion with the Father. His authority came from the Father (cf. Mt 11.27; Jn 14:10–12)" (ARCIC *Gift*, 9). According to the Methodist–Catholic dialogue, "The two divine missions – the sending of the Son and of the Spirit by the Father – are extensions in our world of time of the two eternal processions in the Trinity" (M–C *Singapore*, 7). "The Father is the source and fountainhead. . .Within the Godhead the Son and the Spirit proceed from the unoriginated Father" (M–C *Honolulu,* 10).

b) *Jesus Christ: the Incarnate Word, Lord and Saviour*

11. It is basic for the search for unity that we speak together in the dialogues about Jesus Christ, proclaiming both his divine and human natures and his saving activity. "A fundamental unity in faith exists wherever church and church communities confess Jesus Christ as true God and true man and as only mediator of salvation according to the scriptures to the glory of God, Father, Son, and Holy Spirit" (L–C *Ways*, 26).

In the dialogues, the participants confess that Jesus Christ is *sent by the Father* on a saving mission. "The purpose of the mystery of Christ himself is to make known. . .the infinite wisdom of God" (*Ref I*, 46). Jesus was "sent among us by God the Father to make known and to bring to completion the divine purpose of salvation, the 'mystery of Christ' hitherto hidden and 'now revealed in the Spirit' (Col 1:26 and *Eph* 3:5)" (M–C *Singapore*, 1; cf. ARCIC *Church*, 1; *Salvation*, 1; M–C *Singapore* 1; *Seoul* 55).

Christ is the *Son of the Father* "in whom all things were created. He is the image of the invisible God" (ARCIC *Salvation,* 1). He is God's Son "born of a woman" (ARCIC *Church,* 8). He took flesh "so that we in turn might share the divine nature and so reflect the glory of God" (ARCIC *Salvation*, 1; cf. IARRCUM *GTUM*, 13). He "is God Incarnate, 'God from God, light from light, true God from true God, of one being with the Father' "(M–C *Seoul,* 55 citing the Nicene–Constantinopolitan creed).

Christ is the *Incarnate Word;* he communicates himself to us "in the whole reality of his divinity and humanity – body, mind and will, and at the same time remains the Son who is in the Father as the Father is in him" (*Ref I*, 83). He is "the Second person of the Trinity who has taken flesh" (M–C *Brighton,* 8). "He is the eternal *Logos* or Word who is God from all eternity and who became flesh and lived among us (cf. John 1:1, 14)" (M–C *Seoul*, 55).

We proclaim together that Jesus Christ is *true God and true man*. "The basic work of unification occurs in the incarnation of the Son of God, in whom divinity and humanity are inseparably united in one person. Everything Jesus Christ says, does and suffers lives from this unity and has as its aim 'that all may be one' (John 17:21)" (L–C *Ways,* 10). Though "he was in the form of God . . . [he] emptied himself . . . being born in the likeness of men (Phil 2.6–8). This is why with the church of every age, we confess Jesus Christ as at once true God and true human being, at once one with God and joined in solidarity with humankind" (*Ref II*, 73). "He took flesh so that we in turn might share the divine nature and so reflect the glory of God" (ARCIC *Salvation*, 1).

Jesus Christ is Lord and Saviour. The dialogues repeatedly confess that *in the death and resurrection of Christ, God has brought salvation.* "Christ's death on the cross and his resurrection is the climax of God's saving act for the redemption of the whole world. By his death Christ offered himself once for all in obedience to the Father for the sins of the world (Heb 9:26–28; 10:11f.)" (L–C *Ministry*, 6; cf. *Ways*, 10, 11; *Christ*, 15, *Church and Justification*, 11; M–C *Nairobi*, 2). "The death and resurrection of Christ is the event which reveals who God is, who we are and who Christ is as mediator between God and humankind" (*Ref II*, 68). Thus, "Through Christ's life, death and resurrection, the mystery of God's love is revealed, we are saved from the powers of evil, sin and death, and we receive a share in the life of God. All of this is pure unmerited gift" (ARCIC *Salvation*, 1; cf. *Eucharist*, 5). It is "the cross and resurrection of Christ that supremely reveal him to us, achieving his purpose and making him our Savior" (M–C *Singapore*, 10).

Jesus Christ is the *One Mediator who brings reconciliation* between God and humanity. "Jesus Christ is the only mediator between God and human beings (1 Tim 2:5). Through Christ 'the world is reconciled to the Father in the communion of the Holy Spirit' " (L–C *Ministry*, 6 citing *Accra*, 5*)*. "We confess together that Christ, established as mediator, achieves our reconciliation in all its dimensions: God reconciling humanity, human beings reconciled with each other; and humanity reconciled with God" (*Ref II*, 71; cf. 70). Hence, "because Christ is the one in whom and through whom all things are created and reconciled, the proper relationship between humanity and the rest of creation is restored and renewed in him (Col 1:15–20, Gal 3:27–29; Col 3:11)" (ARCIC *Church,* 9; cf. 15, 22; *Life in Christ,* 4; *Gift,* 9; IARCCUM *GTUM,* 13; L–C *Ways,* 9).

The dialogues affirm the uniqueness of Christ. "Jesus Christ is God's definitive and personal word of grace, transcending God's manifestation of himself through Moses and the prophets" (L–C *Apostolicity,* 432). "As a result of Christ's exaltation, his saving act is valid and effective for the whole of humankind. Jesus Christ is therefore the high priest not just once, but once for all, who intercedes for his flock before the Father for all time (Heb 7:25)" (L–C *Ministry,* 7). "We confess together that just as God is unique, the Mediator and Reconciler between God and humankind is unique and that the fullness of reconciliation is entire and perfect in him. Nothing and nobody could replace or duplicate, complete or in any way add to the unique mediation accomplished 'once for all' (Heb 9:12) by Christ, 'mediator of a new covenant' (Heb 9:15; cf. 8:6 and 12:24)" (*Ref II,* 72). "In the Son, God has spoken definitively to us: the Son who is so completely the expression of his heavenly Father that he is called God's Word (Jn 1:1–18)" (M–C *Singapore,* 9; cf. L–C *Church and Justification,* 10, 11, 19; *Christ,* 17; *Malta,* 48; *Ministry,* 6).

Confession of Jesus Christ as Lord and Saviour. " 'Jesus the Christ' or 'Jesus the Lord' is the original form of the Christian confession of faith. The author of this confession, through which the church as community becomes heard in the world, is the Holy Spirit, in whose power Christ is known as the Lord (1 Cor 12:3), and God the Father, who by his revelation gives us faith in the Messiah and Son (cf. Matt 16:17)" (L–C

Church and Justification, 11). "Thus, in the light of Jesus' resurrection and exaltation, Christians have confessed that he has been made Christ and Lord (cf. Acts 2:36)" (*Ref II,* 73; cf. *Ref I,* 77). "When we confess that Jesus Christ is Lord, we praise and glorify God the Father, whose purpose for creation and salvation is realized in the Son, whom he sent to redeem us and to prepare a people for himself by the indwelling of the Holy Spirit" (ARCIC *Salvation,* 9; cf. *Authority I,* 1). "It is the Cross and Resurrection of Christ that supremely reveal him to us, achieving his purpose and making him our Savior" (M–C *Singapore,* 10; cf. *Rio,* 28 and *Denver,* 56).

It is *Jesus Christ the Incarnate Word who calls the Church into being.* "It is the will of God for the whole creation that all things should be brought to ultimate unity and communion in Christ (Eph 1:10; Col 1:19–20)" (ARCIC *Church,* 15; cf. 22). "The Church takes its shape from the Incarnation from which it originated and the Eucharistic action by which its life is constantly being renewed" (M–C *Nairobi,* 10). "Given the way in which, according to the Scriptures, God has entered human history, the Church's doctrine is centred on Christ. It flows from the identification of Jesus of Nazareth as the Savior expected by Israel, the people of God whose story is told in the Bible" (M–C *Brighton,* 8; cf. *Seoul,* 67).

c) *The Holy Spirit: Lord and giver of life*
12. The Holy Spirit is at once "the *bond of unity* between Father and Son" (L–C *Ways,* 12; italics ours) and the *bond of communion* "uniting individual Christians to Christ and to one another" (M–C *Seoul,* 58). "The Spirit of God is poured into the hearts of believers – the Spirit of adoption, who makes us sons and daughters of God. ... Through baptism we are united with Christ in his death and resurrection, we are by the power of the Spirit made members of one body, and together

we participate in the life of God" (ARCIC *Salvation*, 1). The Holy Spirit "unit(es) local church communities with each other in the one Church of Christ. Within the Church, the Spirit is the bond of communion and connection across both space and time" (M–C *Seoul*, 58; cf. 59).

"The Holy Spirit is *present and active throughout the history of salvation*" (*Ref II*, 75; italics ours). As professed in the Nicene–Constantinopolitan Creed, we jointly affirm that the Holy Spirit is "the Lord, the giver of life". "In the beginning, God's Spirit hovered over the waters of chaos to bring light and life, and was breathed into Adam, God's human creation. The same Spirit inspired the prophets, promising a new beginning, a new creation, a new covenant. In that new beginning, the Holy Spirit overshadowed the Church, bringing the new life promised by Christ, the new Adam" (M–C *Seoul*, 58).

It is especially in the Christ event, and in the continuing life and witness of the body of Christ, that our dialogues have spoken of the presence and work of the Holy Spirit. As testified in the Gospels, most especially in the Gospel of Luke, "During his life on earth, Jesus Christ did all things in the Holy Spirit" (L–C *Eucharist*, 21; cf. M–C *Singapore*, 24). The Reformed–Catholic dialogue offers a helpful overview: "In the life of Jesus the Spirit intervenes at all the decisive moments .. By the life, death and resurrection of Jesus, the Holy Spirit becomes the common gift of the Father and the Son to humanity" (*Ref II*, 75; cf. L–C *Eucharist*, 21 and M–C *Singapore*, 23–26)

Through the power of the Holy Spirit, the Christian community *connects to* and is grounded in *the paschal mystery* and the descent of the Holy Spirit on Jesus' disciples at Pentecost (cf. L–C *Ways*, 12; M–C *Singapore*, 26; *Ref II*, 76,

84; ARCIC *Authority I Elucidation*, 2). "It was in the power of the Spirit that he offered himself as sacrifice (Heb 9:14) and conquered sin and death and rose from the tomb, and lives in the midst of his Pentecost community. Through and in the Spirit Christians are to remain bound to Christ and continue his work" (L–C *Eucharist*, 21). "The Spirit is the power of living communion who makes possible our participation here and now in the saving events of the life, death and rising of Christ" (M–C *Seoul*, 83).

"In Christ, the Holy Spirit renews our hearts and equips and calls us to good works (*JDDJ*, 15)" (L–C *Apostolicity*, 146). "Through the Holy Spirit we become a 'new generation' in Christ (2 Cor 5:17; Gal 6:15)" (L–C *Ministry*, 8). "The Spirit brings newness of life in Christ to the baptized person" (*Ref III*, 128). While the Spirit blows where he wills, working "in such a way as to include people, both within and outside of the church, making use of whatever capacities and limitations they have", the Holy Spirit continues to guide the Church through history (*Ref III*, 195; cf. 136), "build[ing] up the church by bestowing upon it different gifts (*charismata*) for the benefit of the whole body" (*Ref III*, 128). Through the "discernment of spirits", the Holy Spirit leads the Christian community to "new insights into the Christ event and new perspectives to the wider community, inviting it to encounter God anew and to profess anew its faith" (*Ref III*, 125). The Spirit "conforms believers to the image of Christ. Living in the presence of the risen Lord, we know by faith the transforming power of the Holy Spirit and are enabled to live as grateful children of the Father" (M–C *Rio*, 26). "The Spirit is the invisible thread running through the work of the Church in the world, enabling our minds to hear and receive the Word, and giving us tongues to speak the Word (John 14:26; 16:13–14; Acts 4:31)" (M–C *Singapore*, 32; also cited in *Seoul,* 59). "The Holy Spirit is the Witness to Christ in the world (John 15:26), anointing all believers for the work of witness and the proclamation of the Good News of Jesus Christ" (M–C *Seoul,* 59; cf. *Authority I Elucidation,* 2). "Unchanging from generation to generation, the Spirit is the living continuity of the Church" (M–C *Seoul,* 59).

All of our dialogues speak of the Holy Spirit in relation to *transformation and salvation.* "[W]e confess together faith in the Holy Spirit, Lord and giver of life, who is bringing to the whole world the salvation gained by Jesus Christ" (L–C *Apostolicity,* 147). "The Spirit is a principal agent in establishing the kingdom and in guiding the church so that it can be a servant of God's work in this process. ... It is the Spirit who plays the decisive role in leading believers to discern what they should do to serve the fuller realization of the kingdom in particular situations. ... Relating the kingdom instrumentality of the church to the Holy Spirit allows us to acknowledge together a more historical and dynamic vision of the church as 'sacrament of the kingdom of God' " (*Ref III,* 195). "Participation in the glory of God, through the mediation of the Son, in the power of the Spirit is the Gospel hope (cf. 2 Corinthians 3:18; 4:4–6)" (ARCIC *Mary,* 52). "The Spirit is God's Gift of Himself to His people. ... He is the love of God reaching out to humankind for its transformation and salvation" (M–C *Honolulu,* 11). The relationship between the Holy Spirit, the Church and the kingdom of God will be treated in greater detail in Chapter Three.

D. Reflections on Chapter One

13. With joy and gratitude we can state that the reports of the four bilateral dialogues indicate a fundamental common

understanding of the Gospel of our Lord Jesus Christ, common creedal faith, shared fundamental convictions about the Holy Trinity, and the salvific action of the persons of the Trinity. In sum, there is fundamental consensus about the Trinity – the core, the foundation, and the ultimate goal of Christian faith. There is also consensus on Jesus Christ, God's incarnate Son, our Lord and Saviour. What we share in faith is therefore much more than what divides us. The common ground we share can be a solid basis to overcome the divisions between us.

While the dialogues have expressed a fundamental common understanding of the Gospel, longstanding differences concerning the Church require us to consider the relationship between Gospel and Church, as will be done in Chapter Three. This discrepancy applies also to the issue of the binding character of our common creeds. The notion of *Sola Scriptura* held that the Bible alone was considered the norm and rule of faith, while the creeds and dogmas were considered merely witnesses to the faith, valid because and insofar as (*quia et quatenus*) they are in harmony with the Scriptures (BC 769). They have to be tested against the Scriptures (cf. IARCCUM *GTUM*, 29). The Reformed tradition goes even further; unlike the Lutheran tradition, it does not have universal Confessional Writings, but adapts and renews its Confessions according to new circumstances, as in the Barmen Declaration (cf. *Ref I*, 37 and *Ref II*, 139).

Since the Enlightenment and the rise of historical methods of exegesis, not only have the Reformers' principles of the clarity and 'self-interpretation' of the Scriptures been called into question, but sometimes even the binding character of the Creeds. Even when a church affirms the Creeds in principle and holds them as their basis, sometimes individual elements of it (e.g., the Virgin Birth) are criticised. Some go even further and call into question the divinity or the bodily resurrection of Jesus Christ. Accordingly, together we have to strengthen the basis of our common faith in the living triune God and give witness to him. Without belief in the Godhead of Jesus Christ, in the salvific meaning of the cross and in the resurrection of Christ, all the rest is without substance and foundation.

What we need first and foremost is basic ecumenism, i.e., renewed common comprehension and appreciation of our common faith as expressed in our common creedal formulas. At this point fundamental questions for future dialogue arise. In particular, we meet here the questions of theological hermeneutics and criteriology, which will accompany us in the chapters which follow.[10]

NOTES

7 For example, the Augsburg Confession states, "The churches among us teach with complete unanimity that the decree of the Council of Nicea ... is true and is to be believed without any doubt" (Art 1; BC 37). In the Smalkald Articles Luther says the "lofty articles of the divine Majesty (*viz. Trinity and Incarnation*) are not matters of dispute or conflict" (BC 300). In the Formula of Concord (1577), Lutherans pledge themselves to hold and defend against contrary teachings the Apostles' Creed, the Nicene Creed, and the Athanasian Creed (BC 486). In his *Institutes of the Christian Religion*, John Calvin expounds on the Apostles' Creed and extensively cites the early Church Fathers in defence of his theological treatise. Calvin's theology connects the believer directly to God in faith, rather than through the historical Church: "A firm and certain knowledge of God's benevolence towards us, founded upon the truth of the freely given promise in Christ, both revealed to our minds and sealed upon our hearts through the Holy Spirit." (*Institutes*, 3.2.7). The Anglican position is set forth in Article VIII of the Thirty Nine Articles: "The Three Creeds, Nicene Creed, Athanasius's Creed, and that which is commonly called the Apostles' Creed,

ought thoroughly to be received and believed: for they may be proved by most certain warrants of Holy Scripture" (1571, reaffirmed 1662). The Lambeth Quadrilateral of 1888 (building on the resolution of the 1886 meeting of the House of Bishops of the Protestant Episcopal Church in the United States of America), identified the "Apostles' Creed, as the Baptismal Symbol; and the Nicene Creed, as the sufficient statement of the Christian faith" among the Articles which provide a basic reconciliation among Christians. Methodism arose as a renewal movement within Anglicanism, and John Wesley in general accepted the doctrine of the Church of England. He refers in a few places to Article VIII in the Church of England's Thirty-Nine Articles, but never questions the dogmatic substance of the Athanasian Creed, although he is troubled by its anathemas (*Ought We to Separate from the Church of England?* 1754-55). The statement of *Wesleyan Essentials of Christian Faith* adopted by the full World Methodist Council at Rio de Janeiro in 1996, includes the sentence "Methodists profess the ancient ecumenical creeds, the Apostles' and the Nicene".

8 The Faith and Order Commission of the WCC has continued to reflect on the basic aspects of faith. An important step towards a common expression of faith was the Study Paper *Confessing the One Faith,* Faith and Order Paper 153 (Geneva 1999). In the United States, this question was dealt with in the Lutheran–Catholic dialogue *The Status of the Nicene Creed as Dogma of the Church* (Lutherans and Catholics in Dialogue I, Augsburg/Minneapolis, 1965), and in the German dialogue in *Glaubensbekenntnis und Kirchengemeinschaft. Modell des Konzils von Konstantinopel (381),* Hrsg. von K. Lehmann–W. Pannenberg (Dialog der Kirchen 1, Freiburg i. Br./Göttingen, 1982).

9 The intimately linked question of the *Filioque* clause was not an issue in the dialogues. It was, however, dealt with in the Klingenthal consultations (1978/79): L. Vischer ed., *Spirit of God – Spirit of Christ: Ecumenical Reflections on the Filioque Controversy* (Geneva 1981).

10 On the hermeneutical problem in multilateral context: *Treasure in Earthen Vessels. An Instrument for an Ecumenical Reflection on Hermeneutics,* Faith and Order Paper 182 (Geneva 1998).

Chapter Two

Salvation, Justification, Sanctification

INTRODUCTION

14. It is the salvific will of God, Father, Son and Holy Spirit, to reconcile to himself all humanity which had turned away from Him through sin, to set creation free from its bondage to decay, and to draw anew all humankind into communion with Himself. Besides 'justification', the Bible uses a variety of terms for this fundamental message: Kingdom of God, salvation, reconciliation, redemption, forgiveness, sanctification, grace, new life, new creation, rebirth – and others. Although justification means the whole of this salvific process, it expresses the fundamental message of the Gospel under a specific juridical–forensic aspect: God by His mercy declares the sinner righteous and thus makes him effectively righteous. In the biblical sense justification means the creative and redeeming action and gift of God, which humans cannot obtain for themselves.

Accordingly, justification of sinful and lost humanity is at the heart of the Gospel. It touches the fundamental truth of our human condition and answers the question about how we as human beings are saved: not by our own means and our good works but by what Jesus Christ has done for us, and what He is for us.

15. Justification became the central issue of the Reformation. The starting point of the whole dispute was the controversy on indulgences, which raised the question of the importance of good works for salvation/justification. Martin Luther perceived the original meaning of justification in Romans 1:17 not as active justification by us, but as a passive gracious endowing of justification by God *sola fide* and *sola gratia*. This was for him the decisive breakthrough, and the liberating answer to his own existential problem. This insight gave him personal assurance of salvation *(Heilsgewißheit)* and became for him the centre, the criterion, and the whole of the Gospel, the doctrine on which the Church stands or falls.

While the question of the nature of justification was dramatically raised by Luther, it was taken up in various forms by other Reformation movements. Calvin agreed with Luther, but for him justification was not the over-arching principle; he saw justification in a pneumatological perspective and was not so much concerned about its existential dimension as about God's sovereignty and honour. For Anglicans justification did not become the central issue, whereas Methodists were more concerned with personal sanctification.

The interpretation of justification given by Luther and Calvin raised fundamental problems on the Catholic side, and gave rise to intense controversies. The different perceptions of Catholics and Protestants led to mutual condemnations, on the Catholic side by the Council of Trent, notably in its *Decree on Justification* (1547). Among other questions, the Council highlighted especially the effective – not just forensic – character of justification, human cooperation, and the meaning of good works, rejecting the Lutheran understanding of the assurance of salvation.

The central and fundamental importance of this question accounts for the passionate debate in the Reformation era on this issue. All the more reason why the recent basic consensus on justification achieved by Lutherans and Catholics is one of the most important ecumenical achievements of the last decades, with consequences touching every aspect of the Christian faith. The Methodist World Conference subsequently associated itself with this consensus, thus enhancing the agreement by bringing out even more forcefully the connection between justification and sanctification.

A. Basic Consensus on Justification

16. The consensus on basic truths of the doctrine of justification in the *Joint Declaration on the Doctrine of Justification (JDDJ)* was formally acknowledged by the Catholic Church and the Lutheran World Federation through an *Official Common Statement* in 1999 and joined by the World Methodist Council in the *Statement of Association with the Joint Declaration on the Doctrine of Justification* in 2006. This achievement was prepared by a long process of Lutheran–Roman Catholic dialogue beginning with *The Gospel and the Church* (1972), and more explicitly in the US Lutheran–Roman Catholic document *Justification by Faith* (1983), as well as the report of the International Lutheran–Roman Catholic Commission on Unity *Church and Justification* (1993), and the German document *The Condemnations of the Reformation Era: Do They Still Divide?* (1994).

1. The Essential Points of the Joint Declaration

a) Basic common understanding of justification

17. The Declaration's presentation of the biblical message of

justification (8-12) begins by citing John 3:16 on God's salvific love in Christ. After reviewing Old Testament preparations of the message, four dense paragraphs (9-12) set forth the rich variety of New Testament expressions for God's work of justifying sinful human beings by his grace through faith.

Paragraphs 15–17 present the heart of the consensus in faith on justification: Lutherans, Methodists and Catholics are one in a shared confession of faith concerning God's justifying work, which occurs because of Christ and through the Holy Spirit:

> "In faith we together hold the conviction that justification is the work of the triune God. The Father sent his Son into the world to save sinners. The foundation and presupposition of justification is the incarnation, death, and resurrection of Christ. Justification thus means that Christ himself is our righteousness, in which we share through the Holy Spirit in accord with the will of the Father. Together we confess: By grace alone, in faith in Christ's saving work and not because of any merit on our part, we are accepted by God and receive the Holy Spirit, who renews our hearts while equipping and calling us to good works" (15).

> "All people are called by God to salvation in Christ. Through Christ alone are we justified, when we receive this salvation in faith. Faith is itself God's gift through the Holy Spirit who works through word and sacrament in the community of believers and who, at the same time, leads believers into that renewal of life which God will bring to completion in eternal life" (16).

> "We also share the conviction that the message of justification directs us in a special way towards the heart of the New Testament witness to God's saving action in Christ: it tells us that as sinners

our new life is solely due to the forgiving and renewing mercy that God imparts as a gift and we receive in faith, and never can merit in any way" (17).

b) *Compatibility in aspects of justification*

18. The *JDDJ* moves on to explicate the basic common understanding of justification in paragraphs 19-39 under seven headings. On each topic, the Declaration shows how points of doctrine apparently dividing Lutherans and Catholics can be understood, after more detailed examination of each tradition, as being open to one another and not destroying the consensus regarding basic truths in each area. Different languages, explanations, and emphases may in fact coexist and even enhance each other.

(1) Although some divergent aspects on the question of personal cooperation remain, paragraphs 19-21 show agreement on human beings being under God's judgment upon their sin:

"We confess together that all persons depend completely on the saving grace of God for their salvation. The freedom they possess in relation to persons and the things of this world is no freedom in relation to salvation, for as sinners they stand under God's judgment and are incapable of turning by themselves to God to seek deliverance, of meriting their justification before God, or of attaining salvation by their own abilities. Justification takes place solely by God's grace" (19).

(2) Paragraphs 22-24 indicate a compatibility between Lutheran insistence on God's declaration of forgiveness and Catholic teaching on the effectiveness of God's grace imparted in justification:

"We confess together that God forgives sin by grace and at the same time frees human beings from sin's enslaving power and imparts the gift of new life in Christ. When persons come by faith to share in Christ, God no longer imputes to them their sin and through the Holy Spirit effects in them an active love. These two aspects of God's gracious action are not to be separated, for persons are by faith united with Christ, who in his person is our righteousness (1 Cor 1:30): both the forgiveness of sin and the saving presence of God himself" (22).

(3) Paragraphs 25-27 show the compatibility of the Lutheran account of justification "by faith" and Catholic teaching on justification "through grace":

"We confess together that sinners are justified by faith in the saving action of God in Christ. By the action of the Holy Spirit in baptism, they are granted the gift of salvation, which lays the basis for the whole Christian life. They place their trust in God's gracious promise by justifying faith, which includes hope in God and love for him. Such a faith is active in love and thus the Christian cannot and should not remain without works. But whatever in the justified precedes or follows the free gift of faith is neither the basis of justification nor merits it" (25).

(4) Paragraphs 28-30 take up the question of the justified person as still affected by sin, and so engaged in an ongoing struggle, praying daily for forgiveness and being continually called to conversion:

"We confess together that in baptism the Holy Spirit unites one with Christ, justifies, and truly renews the person. But the justified must all through life constantly look to God's unconditional justifying grace. They also are continuously exposed to the power of sin still pressing its attacks (cf. Rom

6:12–14) and are not exempt from a lifelong struggle against the contradiction to God within the selfish desires of the old Adam (cf. Gal 5:16; Rom 7:7–10). The justified also must ask God daily for forgiveness as in the Lord's Prayer (Mt. 6:12; 1 Jn 1:9), are ever again called to conversion and penance, and are ever again granted forgiveness" (28).

— (5) Paragraphs 31-33, on law and Gospel in justification, indicate a Lutheran-Catholic agreement that by Christ's death and resurrection, central in the Gospel, the observance of the law has been set aside as a way to salvation through meritorious works:

"We confess together that persons are justified by faith in the gospel "apart from works prescribed by the law" (Rom 3:28). Christ has fulfilled the law and by his death and resurrection has overcome it as a way to salvation. We also confess that God's commandments retain their validity for the justified and that Christ has by his teaching and example expressed God's will which is a standard for the conduct of the justified also" (31).

— (6) Paragraphs 34-36 show that assurance of salvation is not a church-dividing difference, because one may never doubt God's mercy in Christ:

"We confess together that the faithful can rely on the mercy and promises of God. In spite of their own weakness and the manifold threats to their faith, on the strength of Christ's death and resurrection they can build on the effective promise of God's grace in Word and Sacrament and so be sure of this grace" (34).

— (7) Finally, paragraphs 37-39 treat the good works of those justified by faith and grace, which are the 'good fruit' indicated by Scripture and the consequence of freely given justification:

> *"We confess together that good works – a Christian life lived in faith, hope and love – follow justification and are its fruits. When the justified live in Christ and act in the grace they receive, they bring forth, in biblical terms, good fruit. Since Christians struggle against sin their entire lives, this consequence of justification is also for them an obligation they must fulfil. Thus both Jesus and the apostolic Scriptures admonish Christians to bring forth the works of love" (37).*

c)   Conclusion on the mutual condemnations

19. What the previous sections have expressed and explained leads to a significant conclusion affecting the relationships between the churches involved, since they have carried through centuries, as part of their official doctrine, a number of mutual condemnations of each other's doctrinal errors on justification. The Declaration states the new light in which these condemnations appear:

> *"The teaching of the Lutheran churches presented in this Declaration does not fall under the condemnations of the Council of Trent. The condemnations in the Lutheran Confessions do not apply to the teaching of the Roman Catholic Church presented in this Declaration" (41).*

Thus, in interacting with each other in further doctrinal dialogue and development of collaborative relations, Lutherans and Catholics are not burdened by official declarations that the other community teaches error on justification.

d)   Issues for further work toward visible unity

20. The *JDDJ* was drafted, approved, and through an official

common statement signed as a milestone in ecumenical efforts toward church unity. The agreement that it formulates as consensus on basic truths and reconciliation of differences remains, however, only one part, albeit a central part, of what must be worked out before the signatory churches can formally declare their readiness to live in full communion and visible unity.

The Declaration itself speaks in paragraph 43 of the imperatives that its shared understanding of God's justifying work be deepened and that this come to exert influence on the life and teaching of the churches involved. Also its conclusions will, one hopes, become the basis for clarifying further issues of doctrine, including some of major importance. The text names some of these points of needed ongoing dialogue:

> *"These include, among other topics, the relationship between the Word of God and church doctrine, as well as ecclesiology, ecclesial authority, church unity, ministry, the sacraments, and the relation between justification and social ethics. We are convinced that the consensus we have reached offers a solid basis for this clarification"* *(43).*

The relation between justification and Church and the ecclesiological consequences of the basic consensus on justification were further developed in *Church and Justification* (1993). The Church is *creatura Evangelii* and at the same time *ministra Evangelii* (cf. L–C *Justification,* 36–40). This will be elucidated in Chapter Three.

2. Towards a Wider Consensus on the Doctrine of Justification

21. The international dialogues between the Catholic Church and the World Alliance of Reformed Churches, and the Anglican–Roman Catholic International Commission, have both produced statements on justification which show many similarities with the presentation of the *JDDJ*. This is illustrated by the following examples, corresponding to the *JDDJ's* strong Trinitarian and Christological foundation, its confession of our complete dependence on God's saving grace for salvation, and its position on "good works".

    In the Reformed–Catholic report *Towards a Common Understanding of the Church* (1990), paragraphs 77–79 present a common synthesis of the understanding of "Justification By Grace, through Faith" following a lengthy "Common Confession of Faith" concerning Jesus Christ as "The Only Mediator Between God and Humankind" (64–76). The Reformed–Catholic report states that "our justification is a totally gratuitous work accomplished by God in Christ" (*Ref II*, 77). Just as the *JDDJ* states that "the foundation and presupposition of justification is the incarnation, death and resurrection of Christ" (15), the Reformed–Catholic report indicates that "the raising to life, by God alone, of Jesus Christ, put to death by all, is the eschatological event which defines faith as reception of a gift of God, not as any human work (Eph 2.8–10)" and that "[w]e receive from Christ our justification" (*Ref II*, 78). ARCIC states agreement "that the act of God in bringing salvation to the human race ... is due solely to the mercy and grace of God, mediated and manifested through Jesus Christ in his ministry, atoning death and rising again" (ARCIC *Salvation*, 3). Working from a Trinitarian perspective, the ARCIC text adds, "The Holy Spirit makes the fruits of

Christ's sacrifice actual within the Church through Word and Sacrament: our sins are forgiven, we are enabled to respond to God's love, and we are conformed to the image of Christ" (ARCIC *Salvation*, 9).

Just as in the *JDDJ* "we confess together that all persons depend completely on the saving grace of God for their salvation" (19), so too in the Reformed–Catholic dialogue "we confess that the acceptance in faith of justification is itself a gift of grace. By the grace of faith we recognize in Jesus of Nazareth . . . the one who saves us . . ." (*Ref II*, 77). "[F]aith is above all a reception. . . . By faith, we are liberated from our presumption that we can somehow save ourselves" (*Ref II, 78*). According to ARCIC, "The Church, as the community of the justified, is called to embody the good news that forgiveness is a gift to be received from God and shared with others" (*Salvation*, 30). God sent us his only Son "to do for us what we could not do for ourselves" (*Salvation*, 18). Sharing in the Kingdom of God "is a gift depending wholly on divine grace". Christians "do not trust in their own merits but in Christ's" (*Salvation*, 23).

Just as in the *JDDJ* "we confess together that good works – a Christian life lived in faith, hope and love – follow justification and are its fruits" (37; cf. 25), so too, according to the Reformed–Catholic dialogue, "the person justified by the free gift of faith . . . can henceforth live according to righteousness" and "is called to bear fruits worthy of that grace" (*Ref II*, 79). According to ARCIC, "Faith is no merely private and interior disposition, but by its very nature is acted out: good works necessarily spring from a living faith (Jas 2:17ff.). They are truly good because, as the fruit of the Spirit, they are done in God, in dependence on God's grace. . . . [W]hile we are not saved because of works, we are created in Christ for good works" (ARCIC *Salvation*, 19).

ARCIC's *Salvation and the Church* corresponds closely with other aspects of justification expressed by the *JDDJ*. For example, the ARCIC text speaks of "the paradox that we are at once just and sinners" (15), paralleling the *JDDJ*'s treatment of 'The Justified as Sinner'. Again, the *JDDJ* speaks of justification at one and the same time involving God's forgiveness and our being made righteous. The ARCIC text notes that "[t]he remission of sins is accompanied by a present renewal, the rebirth to newness of life. ... God sanctifies as well as acquits us" (ARCIC *Salvation*, 18). In particular, it highlights the intimate relation between justification and the Church as sign, steward and instrument of God's design and foretaste of God's Kingdom in a world full of suffering and injustice, division and strife (cf. ARCIC *Salvation*, 25–31). "Thus the message of the Church is not a private pietism irrelevant to contemporary society, nor can it be reduced to a political or social programme. Only a reconciled and reconciling community, faithful to its Lord, in which human divisions are being overcome, can speak with full integrity to an alienated, divided world, and so be a credible witness to God's saving action in Christ and a foretaste of God's kingdom" (ARCIC *Salvation*, 30).

B. JUSTIFICATION AND SANCTIFICATION

22. Justification is closely linked with sanctification and with other vital aspects of life in Christ. The *JDDJ* includes language expressive of sanctification, without using that word. While there is no claim in the *JDDJ* that there is consensus on the question of sanctification, or on its relation to justification, there is much agreement on this across these four dialogues. The World Methodist Council's statement of association with the *JDDJ* explicitly addresses the relationship

between justification and sanctification, expressing strong Methodist convictions concerning this relationship.

After recalling this, we look to the bilateral dialogues which address the subject, where we find similar language concerning the relationship between justification and sanctification.

The *JDDJ* states that "by grace alone, in faith in Christ's saving work ... we ... receive the Holy Spirit, who renews our hearts while equipping and calling us to good works" (15). The Holy Spirit "truly renews the person" [28]. "When persons come by faith to share in Christ, ... the Holy Spirit effects in them an active love" (22); the text adds that "such a faith is active in love and thus the Christian cannot and should not remain without works" (25). "The justified ... are ever again called to conversion and penance, and are ever again granted forgiveness" (28).

Crucial for Methodists is "the deep connection between forgiveness of sins and making righteous, between justification and sanctification" (*Statement of Association with the JDDJ*, 4.2). Salvation reflects a twofold action of God's grace: "By justification we are saved from the guilt of sin and restored to the favour of God; by sanctification we are saved from the power and root of sin, restored to the image of God" (4.2, citing John Wesley, Sermon 85, II.1). "Methodist theology has tried to take seriously Paul's assertion: 'Now that you have been freed from sin and enslaved to God, the return you get is sanctification and its end, eternal life' (Romans 6:22)" (4.4) Thus Wesley "developed the doctrine of 'Christian perfection' or 'entire sanctification' (cf. 1 Thessalonians 5:23)" (4.4). The Methodist *Statement of Association with the JDDJ* outlines the core content of this concept, which John Wesley "considered to be at the heart of Methodist teaching" (4.4).

The Methodist–Catholic dialogue also addresses the relationship between justification and sanctification in its bilateral reports (cf. M–C *Honolulu*, 13; *Singapore*, 39).

The Reformed–Catholic dialogue states that "justification by faith brings with it the gift of sanctification, which can grow continuously as it creates life, justice and liberty. Jesus Christ, the one mediator between God and mankind, is also the unique way which leads toward pleasing God. Faith receives freely and bears testimony actively, as it works itself out through love (Gal 5.6)" (*Ref II,* 79).

According to ARCIC, "justification and sanctification are two aspects of the same divine act (1 Cor 6:11)". This means that "when God promises the removal of our condemnation and gives us a new standing before him, this justification is indissolubly linked with his sanctifying recreation of us in grace" (ARCIC *Salvation,* 15). "Sanctification is that work of God which actualizes in believers the righteousness and holiness without which no one may see the Lord" (ARCIC *Salvation,* 17). "God's declaration of forgiveness and reconciliation does not leave repentant believers unchanged but establishes with them an intimate and personal relationship. The remission of sins is accompanied by a present renewal, the rebirth to newness of life.... God sanctifies as well as acquits us" (ARCIC *Salvation*, 18).

C. REFLECTIONS ON CHAPTER TWO

23. The dialogue on the doctrine of justification has brought Catholics, Lutherans and Methodists to agreement on elements important for unity in faith. This result is an important step on the road to full communion, and a milestone in ecumenical

relations. It is indeed a permanent achievement. Catholics, ➤ Lutherans and Methodists have reached substantive agreement on what was once the central ecumenical problem, with consequences for every aspect of Christian faith and life.

As detailed above, the *JDDJ* itself identified questions where further clarification is needed (cf. 43). This is especially true in relation to deepening the biblical foundation of the doctrine of justification.[11] Further discussion is also needed on the question of indulgences as the starting point of the dispute on justification.[12] Moreover, certain issues which have been substantially resolved by the *JDDJ* could nevertheless benefit from further explanation and clarification, such as different perspectives on *simul iustus et peccator*, the role of penance in Christian life, or human cooperation – the extent to which human beings cooperate with God in justification.[13] The ecclesiological problems connected with justification, often missed in the *JDDJ*, were extensively dealt with in the Lutheran–Catholic Dialogue *Church and Justification* (1993), and Chapter Three here offers further clarifications. It is clear that continued reflection is required on all these questions.

An ongoing tension exists in relation to paragraph 18 of the *JDDJ*, where it is said that Lutherans emphasize the unique importance of justification as the criterion which "serves to orient all the teaching and practice of our churches to Christ", whereas Catholics are "bound by several criteria". With this affirmation Catholics want to see the doctrine and the criterion of justification integrated into the whole context of Christology and Trinity, as well as into the ecclesiological context, as expressed in the creedal formulas. The Second Vatican Council speaks in this context of the hierarchy of truths (*UR* 11) as a hermeneutical principle.[14] Here we are confronted again with the hermeneutics and the criteriology of our creedal formulas and their binding character. Misinterpretation of what is stated in paragraph 18 of the *JDDJ* can lead to further misunderstanding about what is required for full communion and about the need to resolve remaining issues.

In the final analysis, the doctrine of justification and sanctification raises the question of theological anthropology and, today, of Christian ethics as the fruit of justification and of the new life of grace.[15] In this respect, new questions -- unknown to the Reformation – have emerged in the modern era, especially regarding personal ethics in questions of marriage and the family, human sexuality, and recent questions of bioethics. These new issues are often divisive not just between Catholics and Protestants or Anglicans, but also *within* these communities themselves.

A renewed understanding of justification has had a progressive impact on questions of political and social ethics, as has been reflected upon especially by ARCIC's *Salvation and the Church* (cf. 30). By the unconditional gracious justification of the sinner God restores the dignity of every person, where 'dignity' is more than the sum of his or her good or bad deeds. The Church as communion of those who are reconciled with God can, and should, be a sign and instrument of reconciliation and peace, an agent of justice and compassion in the face of sin and the structures of sin in society.

The positive outcome of the dialogues up to now gives us hope that further consensus on justification and theological anthropology can be achieved, and that the ecumenical questions recently raised in this context can be faced in serious, open and Spirit–led discussion.

NOTES

11 In the meantime the biblical foundations of the doctrine of justification were more explicitly and profoundly discussed by a Lutheran–Catholic group of biblical scholars meeting at St Paul's Outside the Walls in 2008 at a conference on the theme 'The Biblical Basis of the Message of Justification'.

12 In order to discuss the question of indulgences within the context of the sacrament of penance the PCPCU invited Catholic, Lutheran and Reformed theologians to a symposium in Rome in 2001. From the Catholic side, the new basis of dialogue on this issue was provided by the Apostolic Constitution of Pope Paul VI *Indulgentiarum Doctrina* (1967).

13 Further deepening and clarifications in the German dialogue: *Lehrverurteilungen – kirchentrennend?* II. Hrsg. von K. Lehmann (Dialog der Kirchen, 5), Freiburg i. Br./Göttingen 1989; *Lehrverurteilungen – kirchentrennend?* IV. Hrsg. von W. Pannenberg und Th. Schneider (Dialog der Kirchen, 8). Freiburg i. Br./ Göttingen 1994, 25-50; *Gerecht und Sünder zugleich. Ökumenische Klärungen.* Hrsg. von Theodor Schneider und Günther Wenz (Dialog der Kirchen, 11) Freiburg i. Br./Göttingen 2001.

14 Cf. Joint Working Group (JWG) between the WCC and the Roman Catholic Church study document entitled *The Notion of 'Hierarchy of Truths': An Ecumenical Interpretation* (1990).

15 On moral issues: the Anglican–Catholic dialogue: *Life in Christ: Morals, Communion and the Church* (1994); the Joint Working Group: *The Ecumenical Dialogue on Moral Issues. Potential Sources of Common Witness or Divisions* (1995). On anthropology in a multilateral context: *Christian Perspectives on Theological Anthropology. A Faith and Order Study Document,* Faith and Order Paper 199 (Geneva 2005).

Chapter Three

The Church

24. The Reformers understood themselves as being in continuity
     with the Tradition of the one, holy, catholic and apostolic
     Church, but their concerns regarding justification and God's
     gracious sovereignty in justifying the sinner gave rise to a
     series of questions about the Church. As early as 1517, Martin
     Luther's dispute about indulgences had given rise to
     controversy about the authority of the Pope and the
     Councils, the power of the keys of the Kingdom, and the
     Gospel as the true treasure of the Church. During the debate
     with Cardinal Cajetan, Luther stated that the Pope does not
     subject himself to the Word of God, but hinders its
     preaching. As a result Luther subsequently came to consider
     the Pope as the Anti-Christ of 2 Thess 2:1-12.

     Luther understood the Church as the congregation of the
     faithful (or *communio sanctorum)* and as the community
     wherein God's word is correctly preached and the sacraments
     are duly administered according to the Gospel (CA VII). The
     Church is *creatura Evangelii* (WA 2,430) and therefore
     subordinate to the Gospel. Her mystery is hidden from the
     world, but the Church is not simply invisible, and is not a
     Platonica civitas (Apol. VII and VIII). She is recognisable by
     signs and marks such as the preaching of the Word of God,

baptism, the sacrament of the altar, the power of the keys, and ministries of the public preaching of the Gospel.

Calvin and the Reformed community "shared the same fundamental concerns: to affirm the sole headship of Jesus Christ over the Church; to hear and proclaim the message of the Gospel as the one Word of God which alone brings authentic faith into being; to re-order the life, practice and institutions of the Church in conformity with the Word of God revealed in Scripture" (*Ref II,* 18). The Reformed–Catholic dialogue summarises the concerns of the reformers which led them to reject anything "in the life of the Church which, in their understanding, obscured the unique mediatorship of Jesus Christ and seemed to give to the Church an excessive role alongside Him. The emphasis placed in the ensuing controversy on the authority of the Church and its hierarchy led them to question the value of episcopal succession as an expression of the continuity of the Church in the apostolic truth through the centuries. In particular, they rejected teachings such as the following: the appeal to the Church's tradition as an authority equal to Scripture or belonging together with it; the universal authority of the Pope; the claim that Church Councils constitute an infallible teaching authority; the canonical distinction between the office of a bishop and that of any other minister of the Word and Sacraments" (*Ref II,* 20).

In the sixteenth century the Church of England asserted its autonomy under God as a local expression of the universal Church. The Elizabethan settlement of the Church of England incorporated both conservative elements (for example, episcopacy was acknowledged to be an indispensable part of the foundations of the Anglicanism) and ideas of the Continental reform movement. The tensions between Catholic and Protestant tendencies in Anglicanism have posed grave questions of unity and identity within the worldwide Anglican communion several times in its history, and particularly so today. While the origins of the Anglican Communion (which gradually developed in the nineteenth century alongside British colonial expansion and Anglican missionary activity) and the reform movement within it are somewhat different from those of the Continental reform, it is notable that they too enshrine ecclesiological differences with respect to the Catholic tradition, especially around the question of the ministry of primacy.

Methodism began as a renewal and a Biblical-oriented spiritual movement within the Church of England, with a strong missionary commitment. John Wesley (1703-91) did not want to separate from the Church of England, but such separation was inevitable when large numbers of unchurched people unconnected to the state-established Church entered the movement. For such people Wesley created ministerial structures parallel to the Anglican authority, so that without a formal act of separation an autonomous Church came into existence. While this new movement was not indifferent to church structures, it was more concerned to emphasise holiness in inspiring and organising a movement for church renewal and mission.

Protestant pietism of the seventeenth and eighteenth centuries held a more subjective ecclesiology, wherein Christianity was perceived as a religion of the heart, and fellowship consisted in a warm personal relationship with Christ and with one's fellow Christians. It held that the Church consists of true believers everywhere. In contrast to such a spiritual understanding of Christian life and of the invisible unity of the Church, the ecumenical movement holds to the goal of the visible unity of the Church.[16]

Whereas traditional polemics and apologetic theology insisted on the *visibility* of the Church over against its *hiddenness,* and disputed mostly about its institutional dimension, the Second Vatican Council in the Dogmatic Constitution on the Church *Lumen gentium* (1964) pointed to the mystery of the Church as people of God, Body of Christ, Temple of the Holy Spirit and laid the foundations for a renewal of the understanding of the Church as *communion*. It emphasized that the Church is one complex reality, which coalesces from a divine and a human element. Following this, a rapprochement with the different Protestant ecclesial traditions became possible. The four dialogues have shown that although fundamental open questions remain in ecclesiology, there are also many convergences and many points in common.[17]

A. COMMON PERSPECTIVES ON THE NATURE AND MISSION OF THE CHURCH

25. Three of the four bilateral dialogues on the Church have been undertaken in light of division stemming from the sixteenth century, and in a situation which has included a strong need for a healing of memories especially in regard to our respective understandings of the Church. It is only in the dialogue with the Methodists, a world communion emerging in the eighteenth century, that the partners have felt less urgency for a healing of memory, and have been able to emphasize more freely common aspects of the Church. Naturally, since the dialogues start from different historical points of departure, they have addressed the question of the nature and mission of the Church in different ways and with different emphases; even when addressing many of the same themes, they have employed different perspectives. As a result, to this point no consistent systematic understanding of

the Church has emerged. ARCIC alone has come closest to producing a full systematic treatment of the Church, while L-C *Church and Justification* is seen by some as an ecclesiology-in-miniature. Mindful of these limitations, nevertheless in all four dialogues common perspectives and many convergences on the nature and mission of the Church can be identified.

1. The Trinitarian Basis of the Church

26. At the outset the four dialogues agree on the Trinitarian roots of the Church. Thus, "Catholics and Lutherans are in agreement that the saving activity of the triune God calls and sanctifies believers through audible and visible means of grace which are mediated in an audible and visible ecclesial community" (L–C *Church and Justification*, 147; cf. 1 and 5; cf. also *Unity*, 57). "The church is ordered through baptism, in which all who believe in Christ are not only washed and signed by the triune God, but are 'built into a spiritual house, to be a holy priesthood' (1 Pet 2:5)" (*Ref II*, 134; cf. *Ref II*, 81). "It is communion with the Father, through the Son, in the Holy Spirit which constitutes the people of the New Covenant as the church. . . ." (ARCIC *Church*, 8; cf. *Life in Christ*, 19). "The Church springs from an initiative by the Holy Trinity and belongs to the sphere of God's grace. 'The revelation of the Triune God is the source of the Church's faith, the Church's mission, and the Church's sacramental life' " (M–C *Seoul*, 52 citing *Rio*, 4; cf. *Seoul* 49, 51).

a) *The Church, the People of God called by God the Father*
27. All the dialogues see the Church in the context of the whole of salvation history as the people of God called by God to be "his people". According to the Lutheran-Catholic dialogue, "The church of the New Testament was always aware that the history of the people of God did not begin with itself. The God

who raised Jesus from the dead is the same God who called Abraham to be the father of all who believe, who elected Israel from among all the nations to be his treasured possession and who entered into an enduring covenant with it (cf. Rom 9:6). In salvation-history the church thus presupposes the history of Israel (cf. Acts 13:16 ff.; Heb 1:1 f.)" (L–C *Church and Justification*, 13; cf. 14–17). "That Jesus as Son of God is the Messiah and that in him the eschatological rule of God has dawned is the unique saving event which effects a definitive salvation for all the nations, going beyond all the saving gifts in the history of his people" (L–C *Church and Justification,* 19).

According to the Reformed-Catholic dialogue, "the church is present at the establishment of the People of the Covenant. Through the law and the prophets, God calls this people and prepares them for a communion which will be accomplished at the sending of Emmanuel, 'God with us' (cf. Mt 1.23)" (*Ref II*, 81). Further, "The church's calling is set within the triune God's eternal plan of salvation for humankind. In this sense, the church is already present at creation (Col 1:15–18). (*Ref II,* 81)."

Salvation history culminates in Christ. "[W]e believe that the coming of Christ, the Word incarnate, brings with it a radical change in the situation of the world in the sight of God. Henceforth the divine gift which God has made in Jesus Christ is irreversible and definitive. On God's side, salvation is accomplished and is offered to all. The presence of God has become inward among believers (Jer 31.33: Ezek 36.26) in a new fashion, by the Holy Spirit which conforms them to the image of Jesus Christ. At the same time, God's presence becomes universal; it is not limited to one people but is offered to all humanity called to be gathered together by Christ in the Spirit" (*Ref II,* 82; cf. 83 and *Ref III,* 46).

The Anglican-Catholic dialogue affirms, "To bring us to union with himself, the Father sent into the world Jesus Christ, his only Son, in whom all things were created" (ARCIC, *Salvation* 1). The dialogue addresses God's will to call us into communion, prefigured in the Abrahamic covenant and realised fully in Christ; "from every period of the long history of the people of Abraham, the books of the Old Testament bear witness to the fact that God wants his people to be in communion with him and with each other... In the fullness of time, God sends his Son, born of a woman, to redeem his people and bring them into a new relationship as his adopted children (cf. Gal 4:4).... It is communion with the Father, through the Son, in the Holy Spirit which constitutes the people of the New Covenant as the Church, 'a people still linked by spiritual ties to the stock of Abraham' (citing Vatican II, *Nostra Aetate*, §4)" (ARCIC *Church*, 7-8). ARCIC adds, "The patriarchs and the prophets received and spoke the word of God in the Spirit. By the power of the same Spirit the Word of God became flesh and accomplished his ministry" (ARCIC *Authority I Elucidation*, 2). "Christ is God's final word to man – his eternal Word made flesh. He is the culmination of the diverse ways in which God has spoken since the beginning (Heb 1 1–3). In him God's saving and revealing purpose is fully and definitively realized" (ARCIC *Authority I Elucidation*, 2).

According to the Methodist-Catholic dialogue, "The Church is a fruit of God's grace, and its nature and mission cannot be understood apart from the mystery of God's loving plan for the salvation of all humanity" (M–C *Seoul,* 49). "Together Catholics and Methodists confess the Church as part of the Triune God's eternal purpose for the salvation of humankind" (M–C *Singapore,* 99). The Methodist-Catholic dialogue, under the heading "People and Family of God the Father", noted that the "Father's overflowing love created humanity for communion with himself" and proceeds to state, "By God's free gift of the covenant, the people of Israel became God's own royal, priestly and prophetic people, chosen to be a light to the nations. By the Father's gift of the new and everlasting covenant, sealed by the blood of Christ, the Lamb of God, those who are 'in Christ' become 'a chosen race, a royal priesthood, a holy nation, God's own people, in order that you may proclaim the mighty acts of him who called you out of darkness into his marvellous light' (1 Peter 2:9).... In Christ, we become the adopted sons and daughters of God the Father, members of his royal and consecrated family, the Church. All of this is the fruit of the outpouring of the Father's creative and gathering love" (M-C *Seoul* 54).

b) *The Church, the Body of Christ*

28. All four dialogues agree that *Jesus Christ founded the Church* and that the Church is built on the foundation of Jesus Christ. Lutherans and Catholics state that " 'No one can lay any foundation other than the one that has been laid; that foundation is Jesus Christ' (1 Cor 3:11). In all its trenchancy this statement is to be evaluated and heeded as the fundamental principle of ecclesiology. 'The one and only foundation of the church is the saving work of God in Jesus Christ which has taken place once for all.' Everything that is to be said on the origin, nature and purpose of the church must be understood as an explanation of this principle" (L–C *Church and Justification*, 10 citing the German dialogue *Kirchengemeinschaft* in *Wort und Sakrament*, 1984). In the same sense Reformed and Catholics affirm, "We therefore confess Jesus Christ as the foundation of the church" (*Ref II*, 83).

In speaking of the apostolicity of the Church, ARCIC notes that "the church is built up by the Spirit upon the foundation of the life, death and resurrection of Christ as these have been witnessed and transmitted by the apostles..." (ARCIC *Church,* 25; cf. 13–14). Methodists and Catholics state, "The church did not create itself: 'It originated in the redemptive act of God in Christ; and it lives in union with Christ's death and resurrection, comforted, guided and empowered by the Holy Spirit'" (M–C *Seoul,* 52 citing *Nairobi,* 3). "As members of Christ's Church, and in communion with Christians throughout the ages, we believe that we continue even today to share in the life and paschal mystery of the incarnate Son, upheld by the Spirit of God" (M–C *Seoul,* 52; cf. *Nairobi,* 2–3).

29. All the dialogues further agree that Jesus Christ stands not only at the beginning of the Church as its founder but is permanently present within his Church, which according to the New Testament witness is *the body of Christ.*

According to Lutherans and Catholics, "As 'body of Christ', the faithful and the church have a share in Christ who was raised from the dead 'by the glory of the Father' (Rom 6:3f.); and through the Holy Spirit the faithful are incorporated into the body of Christ, and they receive their gifts for the building up of the body" (L–C *Church and Justification,* 64; cf. 132). Reformed and Catholics have "full agreement in presenting the church as the Body of Christ" (*Ref I,* 16). "Christ is present in the church and through his lordship over the church, he exercises his lordship over the world" (*Ref I,* 43).

According to ARCIC, "Those who are reconciled to God form 'one body in Christ and are individually members one of another' (Rom 12:5). By the action of the same Spirit, believers are baptized into the one Body (1 Cor 12:13) and in the breaking of the bread they also participate in that one Body (1 Cor 10:16–17; 11:23–29). Thus the Church 'which is Christ's body, the fullness of him who fills all in all', reveals and embodies 'the mystery of Christ' (cf. Eph 1:23; 3:4.8–11" (ARCIC *Church*, 17). According to Methodists and Catholics, the Spirit "creates and maintains the oneness of the Church, bringing the many into unity and joining to their Head the members of the Body of Christ" (M–C *Singapore*, 28). "The diverse gifts in the Body of Christ are complementary, and serve together the Church's communion and connection in love and in truth" (M–C *Brighton* 50; cf. 2, 13).

As a consequence all four dialogues agree that the *Church has its meaning and purpose in Jesus Christ.* "According to Paul, the community ... is in fact 'Christ' (1 Cor 12.12). ... 'The church is subject to Christ' always (Eph 5:24) and linked to him in love (cf. Eph 4.16). The interlinking of unity and diversity becomes clear especially in the image of the bride and bridegroom (cf. 2 Cor 11:2; Eph 5:22ff.; Rev 19:7f.; 21:2; 22:17)" (L–C *Church and Justification*, 132). "The mission and task of Jesus ... are authoritative for the church of every age and culture" (*Ref I,* 14). "The kingdom proclaimed by Jesus provides the context for understanding the nature and mission of the church" (*Ref III,* 64).

In a similar way ARCIC states, "Jesus, as the Word of God, sums up in himself the whole of God's self-disclosure" (ARCIC *Authority I Elucidation,* 2). "The Church is a community which consciously seeks to submit to Jesus Christ" (ARCIC *Authority I,* 4). The Methodist–Roman Catholic dialogue states, "The Church is summoned by the personal call of the Risen Lord. He says to each of us: Come to me, Follow me, and Go in my name. We are transformed by the touch of his presence and become new people, ready and able to follow him and to live a new life in Christ. We are sent forth by him into the world to proclaim with joy the good news of God's love for all humanity, and to 'make disciples of all nations' (Matthew 28:20)" (M–C *Seoul*, 57).

30. Finally, for all the dialogues the active presence of Christ within the Church is the foundation of *the Church's role in salvation*. Here both the Lutheran–Catholic and Reformed–Catholic dialogues speak of the role of the Church in salvation in light of the role of the Church in justification, while Anglican–Catholic and Methodist–Catholic dialogues tend to treat the Church within the context of the history of revelation and salvation.

Lutherans and Catholics jointly state, "Of course the personal relation between Christ and church must not obscure the different quality of relations between the two; for from the start the church is the redeemed, receiving church and remains so forever. Precisely in the light of the doctrine of justification it becomes plain that the church owes its existence and activity solely to the mercy of God in Jesus Christ and to the breath of the Holy Spirit. Only so is Christ able to make salvation effectual through the church in proclamation and the sacraments. Both the Lutheran and Catholic understandings of the church's salvific service through word and sacrament are based on this biblical foundation" (L–C *Church and Justification*, 133).

According to the Reformed–Catholic dialogue, "Together we confess the church, for there is no justification in isolation. All justification takes place in the community of believers, or is ordered toward the gathering of such a community. Fundamental for us all is the presence of Christ in the church, considered simultaneously as both a reality of grace and a concrete community in time and space. Christ himself acts in the church in the proclamation of the Word, in the celebration of the sacraments, in prayer and in intercession for the world. This presence and this action are enabled and empowered by the Spirit, by whom Christ calls to unite human beings to himself, to express his reality through them, to associate them in the mystery of his self-offering for them" (*Ref II*, 80).

ARCIC states that "the Church has been entrusted with the stewardship of the means of grace and with the message of salvation. In the power of Christ's presence through the Spirit it is caught up in the saving mission of Christ. The mandate given to the Church to bring salvation to all the nations constitutes its unique mission. In this way the Church not only signifies the new humanity willed by God and inaugurated by Christ. It is itself an instrument of the Holy Spirit in the extension of salvation to all human beings in all their needs and circumstances to the end of time" (ARCIC *Church*, 22; cf. *Salvation*, 1).

According to the Methodist–Catholic dialogue, "The Risen Christ is present at the heart of the life of his Church, working in and through the Church which he unites with himself as a communal sign and instrument of his saving presence. Only the presence of the Holy Spirit makes it possible for the Church to be a sign or sacrament of the Risen Christ for our whole world" (M–C *Seoul*, 77).

c) *The Church, Temple of the Holy Spirit*

31. According to New Testament witness *the Church is the Temple of the Holy Spirit*. It is the Holy Spirit who binds the faithful to Christ. "In the church as 'temple of the Holy Spirit', it is the Spirit who as the 'Spirit of Christ' (Rom 8:9; cf. 2 Cor 3:17) binds the faithful to Christ, the mediator of all salvific gifts, and who through him gives them access to the Father, whom they may invoke as 'Abba, Father' in the same Spirit" (L–C

Church and Justification, 64). "Just as the Spirit came upon Jesus at the moment of his baptism, so the Spirit descends upon the disciples gathered in the upper room (Acts 2:1–12) and on the Gentiles who listen to the word (Acts 10:44–48). These three closely linked 'Pentecosts' belong to the foundation of the church and make it the 'Temple of the Holy Spirit.' Thus the design pursued from the beginning by God the Creator and saviour – to bring into being a people – is accomplished" (*Ref II,* 76; cf. ARCIC *Church*, 29; M–C *Seoul*, 58–59).

The Holy Spirit actualises the work of Christ in the Church, and guides the Church. "Lutherans and Catholics are convinced that the Holy Spirit unceasingly leads and keeps the church in the truth" (L–C *Malta*, 22), because "God's truth presents itself to believers in the power of the Spirit, for the same Spirit who empowers witnesses to the gospel also makes it possible for others to hear and understand.... This is the Paraclete, the advocate, supporter, exhorter, and comforter, who will abide 'forever' with Jesus' disciples (Jn 14:6), who 'will teach them everything' and remind them of all that Jesus had said to them (14:16). The Spirit will witness on Jesus' behalf (15:26). In his farewell discourse, Jesus states the promise that will accompany the disciples on their mission: 'When the Spirit of truth comes, he will guide you into all the truth' (16:13)" (L–C *Apostolicity*, 312-313).

"The Holy Spirit actualises Christ's work of redemption in the hearts of individuals by bringing about their conversion and regeneration. As such, the Spirit is a principal agent in establishing the kingdom and in guiding the church so that it can be a servant of God's work in this process" (*Ref III,* 195; cf. *Ref I,* 54). "While the kingdom theme takes the world and human effort in history seriously, it does not surrender openness to a transcendent future in the fullness of God. Only

God ultimately can fulfil humankind's deepest aspirations"
(*Ref III,* 184; cf. 185).

"The Spirit, active in the once for all events of the ministry of
Jesus, continues to teach the Church, bringing to remembrance what Christ did and said, making present the fruits of
his redemptive work and the foretaste of the kingdom (cf. Jn
2.22; 14.26)" (ARCIC *Gift,* 18; cf. *Church,* 17). "The Spirit is
the invisible thread running through the work of the Church
in the world, enabling our minds to hear and receive the
Word, and giving us tongues to speak the Word (John 14:26;
16:13–14; Acts 4:31). Relating us to one another and to
Christ our Head, the Holy Spirit gives coherent shape and
variety to the people of God. Within that people as they are,
and for that people as they shall be, the Holy Spirit invites us
all to share in the service of the One who came to serve"
(M–C *Singapore,* 52; cf. *Seoul,* 59).

The Holy Spirit is the bond of communion in the Church.
"Lutherans and Catholics confess 'the communion of saints'
(*sanctorum communionem*) in the Apostles' Creed ... It is a
communion of saints because it lives harmoniously in one
faith and in love under one head, Christ and by the Holy
Spirit. Through the Holy Spirit every member of this 'holy
community' shares in everything and especially in the word of
God. The Holy Spirit constantly remains with the church,
sanctifies it, strengthens its faith and produces its fruits" (L–C
Church and Justification, 291; cf. 293). The Reformed–Catholic
dialogue, speaking about Church's celebration of the presence
of Christ in the sacrament, says that "around this centre, and
with the multiplicity of gifts granted by the Spirit ... it lives as
a *koinonia* of those who need and help each other" (*Ref I,* 54;
cf. *Ref II,* 6).

"It is communion with the Father, through the Son, in the Holy Spirit which constitutes the people of the New Covenant as the Church, 'a people still linked by spiritual ties to the stock of Abraham' " (ARCIC *Church,* 8 citing *Nostra aetate,* 4; cf. IARCCUM *GTUM,* 15; ARCIC *FR Introduction,* 5; *Church,* 13; 43). "The Spirit is the invisible bond of communion (cf. 2 Corinthians 13:13), uniting individual Christians to Christ and to one another, and uniting local church communities with each other in the one Church of Christ. Within the Church, the Spirit is the bond of communion and connection across both space and time" (M–C *Seoul,* 58).

2. The Mission of the Church – Church and the Kingdom of God

a) The Church and the Kingdom of God

32. Each of the four dialogues speaks of the relationship between the Church and the Kingdom of God, and they demonstrate a basic agreement on that relationship. In a particular way, this issue is taken up in the Reformed-Catholic dialogue. "Whoever becomes involved with Jesus becomes involved with the kingdom of God. In this context we have to understand also the coming into being of the community of disciples, rooted in Israel as God's people that witnesses to Jesus and his kingdom in a new way" (*Ref III,* 160; cf. 62, 64 and 163). "The kingdom aims at the transformation of the whole of creation into eternal glory, and the church must be understood in the context of this divine intentionality. Citizenship in the kingdom means an ongoing summons to solidarity with people, particularly with the excluded and oppressed. The kingdom will only mean something to the multitudes that suffer when it is experienced as a transforming power. As Paul writes in 1 Cor 4:20, 'For the kingdom of

God consists not in talk but in power' " (*Ref III*, 180; cf. ARCIC *Salvation*, 31; M-C *Honolulu*, 22).

In a similar way the Lutheran–Catholic dialogue notes that "the church is seen in various ways as sign and instrument of the presence of Christ, the mission of Christ, and the kingdom" (L–C *Church and Justification*, 305). Citing the conference of the Commission on World Mission and Evangelism of the World Council of Churches held in Melbourne (1980), the Lutheran–Catholic dialogue states, "The whole church of God, in every place and time, is a sacrament of the kingdom which came in the person of Jesus Christ and will come in its fullness when he returns in glory" (L–C *Church and Justification*, 305). "Lutherans and Catholics together regard the church as the dawning and the instrument of the kingdom of God. Two things should be maintained together. On the one hand, there is the reality of the powers of the kingdom of God ... On the other hand, there is the interim nature of all words and signs in which salvation is imparted ... To this extent the church always lives on the basis of letting itself be lifted up into the coming kingdom, remembering its own provisional nature. The earthly church will find its eschatological consummation only when the kingdom has come" (L–C *Church and Justification*, 307; cf. 72, 73).

"Patterned according to Christ, the Wisdom of God, and empowered by the Holy Spirit of God, the Church is called, not only to proclaim God's kingdom, but also to be the sign and first-fruits of its coming. The unity, holiness, catholicity and apostolicity of the Church derive their meaning and reality from the meaning and reality of God's kingdom" (ARCIC *Life in Christ*, 19; cf. *Salvation*, 26). In the summary words of ARCIC, "The good news of the Gospel is the coming of the kingdom of God (cf. Mk 1:15), the redemption of the world by our Lord Jesus Christ (cf. Gal 4:4–5), the forgiveness of sins and new life in the Spirit (cf. Acts 2:38), and the hope of glory (cf. Col 1:27)" (ARCIC *Life in Christ*, 17). "The Church which in this world is always in need of renewal and purification, is already here and now a foretaste of God's Kingdom in a world still awaiting its consummation – a world full of suffering and injustice, division and strife" (ARCIC *Salvation*, 30).

According to the Methodist-Catholic dialogue, "Jesus does more than announce and point to the coming kingdom; in his powerful deeds and life of loving obedience to the Father, the kingdom is already present (Luke)" (M–C *Rio*, 17; cf. *Seoul*, 68). "God inaugurated his Kingdom in Christ" (M–C *Honolulu*, 22). "Methodists and Catholics agree that 'in all situations, the underlying truth of the Church's nature and purpose remains the same: by its life and witness the Church *points towards*, by its sharing and worship it *anticipates*, and through its mission it *is an instrument of* the ultimate reality of the Kingdom of God, actualised in Jesus Christ' (CLP, 2.3.19; emphasis added)" (M–C *Seoul*, 77 citing *Called to Love and Praise*; cf. *Singapore*, 65 and 99). "The Church lives between the times of the life, death, resurrection and exaltation of Jesus Christ and his future coming in glory. The Spirit fills the Church, empowering it to preach the word, celebrate the eucharist, experience fellowship and prayer, and carry out its mission to the world: thus the Church is enabled to serve as sign, sacrament and harbinger of the Kingdom of God in the time between the times" (M–C *Nairobi*, 8; cf. ARCIC *Life in Christ*, 20). "The Church in Christ's name and by the power of his Spirit serves the kingdom of God by working to heal and transform the world here and now" (M–C *Seoul*, 68; cf. *Rio*, 79).

While the Church is the foretaste of the Kingdom of God, according to all four dialogues the Church remains a pilgrim Church. Throughout its history its members have struggled with human sinfulness and always will, and because of this the Church as an institution of people here on earth is in need of continual reform. Nevertheless, the holiness of the Church endures as a permanent gift of God in Jesus Christ. God continues to work through the Church, and the Church continues to proclaim God's Kingdom and to witness to the saving activity of Christ, despite the sinfulness of its members.

"Of course, the confession of the church's holiness has always gone hand in hand with the knowledge that the power of evil and sin, although it will not overcome the church, is nevertheless at work in it. The church 'without a spot or wrinkle or anything of the kind' (Eph 5:27) will appear only at the end of its earthly pilgrimage, when 'Christ will present her to himself in all her glory'. The holiness of the church therefore exists both 'already' and 'not yet'. It is a 'genuine though imperfect holiness' " (L–C *Church and Justification,* 153; cf. 146–147, 154–56). "[W]e both recognize that, whatever the effect of sin on persons and institutions, the holiness of the preaching of the Word and of the administration of the sacraments endures, because the gift of God to the church is irrevocable. In this sense the church is holy, for it is the instrument of that gift of holiness which comes from God" (*Ref II,* 122).

"[T]he credibility of the Church's witness is undermined by the sins of its members, the shortcomings of its human institutions, and not least by the scandal of division. The Church is in constant need of repentance and renewal so that it can be more clearly seen for what it is: the one, holy body of Christ. Nevertheless the Gospel contains the promise that despite all failures the Church will be used by God in the achievement of his purpose: to draw humanity into communion with himself and with one another, so as to share his life, the life of the Holy Trinity" (ARCIC *Salvation* 29; cf. *Church,* 21; *Ref III,* 174). "The Church of Christ is a pilgrim community, journeying together from sinfulness to holiness as God in his grace leads us forward. Even though we are still a wandering people, always in need of repentance and renewal, yet we are confident of Christ's promises and the transforming presence of the Holy Spirit. We place our trust in Christ who says to his Church: 'My grace is sufficient for you, for my power is made perfect in weakness' (2 Corinthians 12:9)" (M–C *Seoul,* 95).

b) *The Church as instrument of salvation*

34. Because the Church within sinful history is a foretaste of the kingdom of God, it follows that it has a role in God's eternal plan of salvation, in his eternal design to save all people. This was the case from the beginning. Even in the events recorded in the Old Testament, Christians have seen an anticipation of the Church. This becomes fully clear in the Christ event, which reveals an irreversible and definitive offer of salvation. The Church, founded by Christ, is an instrument of God's offer of salvation, and it was envisioned as such from the beginning; and this remains true of the Church today. The dialogues speak of the Church as an effective instrument of salvation; some of them, as a *sacrament of salvation*, a sacrament of the Kingdom of God.

The Reformed–Catholic dialogue states, "The church's calling is set within the triune God's eternal plan of salvation for humankind. In this sense, the church is already present at creation (Col 1:15–18). It is present in the history of humankind: 'the Church from Abel', as it was called in the ancient church" (*Ref II*, 81). This theme recalls the patristic reflection articulated by Augustine, echoed by *Lumen gentium*, 52. The dialogue does not call into question the continuity of the history of salvation or the significance of God's interventions in the course of Old Testament revelation. "For God has not rejected this people (Rom 11:1). The continued existence of the chosen people is an integral part of the history of salvation" (*Ref II*, 81).

"[W]e believe that the coming of Christ, the Word incarnate, brings with it a radical change in the situation of the world in the sight of God. Henceforth the divine gift which God has made in Jesus Christ is irreversible and definitive. On God's side, salvation is accomplished and is offered to all. The presence of God has become inward among believers (Jer 31.33: Ezek 36.26) in a new fashion, by the Holy Spirit which conforms them to the image of Jesus Christ. At the same time, God's presence becomes universal; it is not limited to one people but is offered to all humanity called to be gathered together by Christ in the Spirit" (*Ref II*, 82; cf. 83 and *Ref III*, 46).

According to the Lutheran–Catholic dialogue, "The church of the New Testament was always aware that the history of the people of God did not begin with itself. ... In salvation-history the church thus presupposes the history of Israel (cf. Acts 13:16ff.; Heb 1:1f.)" (L–C *Church and Justification*, 13; cf. 14–15, 133).

ARCIC notes, "The Church is ... an instrument for the realisation of God's eternal design, the salvation of humanity. While we recognise that the Holy Spirit acts outside the community of Christians, nevertheless it is within the Church, where the Holy Spirit gives and nurtures the new life of the Kingdom, that the Gospel becomes a manifest reality. . . ." (ARCIC *Salvation,* 28). "The Church is therefore called to be, and by the power of the Spirit actually is, a sign, steward and instrument of God's design" (ARCIC *Salvation,* 29).

The Methodist–Catholic dialogue states, "Together Catholics and Methodists confess the Church as part of the Triune God's eternal purpose for the salvation of humankind" (M–C *Singapore,* 99). "The Church is a fruit of God's grace, and its nature and mission cannot be understood apart from the mystery of God's loving plan for the salvation of all humanity" (M–C *Seoul,* 49).

All the four dialogues, each in their own way, emphasize the importance of unity for the Church's effective witness. For example, "Only a reconciled and reconciling community, faithful to its Lord, in which human divisions are being overcome, can speak with full integrity to an alienated, divided world, and so be a credible witness to God's saving action in Christ and a foretaste of God's Kingdom" (ARCIC *Salvation,* 30; cf. *Church,* 20 and 23; *Ref III,* 197; M–C *Seoul,* 62).

c)   *The Church as sacrament of the Kingdom of God*
35.   Some dialogues have described the Church as sacrament of the Kingdom of God. According to the Reformed–Catholic dialogue, "The church is meant to serve the establishment of the kingdom as a prophetic sign and an effective instrument in the hands of God" (*Ref III,* 64). "Through exploring the theme of common witness to the kingdom, Reformed and Catholics have thus been able to discover a further fundamental agreement about the church. We can affirm that the church is a kind of sacrament of the kingdom of God, with a

genuine role of mediation, but only in so far as it is utterly dependent upon God. Our agreement about the church's dependence upon God in Christ through the power of the Holy Spirit gives hope that we have also made some progress in opening the way for greater convergence. By speaking about the church as 'sacrament of the kingdom of God' past tensions regarding differing convictions about the continuity, ministry and order of the church through the ages may prove to be complementary and even creative in shared reconstruction" (*Ref III*, 197; cf. 191 and 194).

The Reformed–Catholic dialogue in its document *Towards a Common Understanding of the Church* (1990) after a lengthy treatment and discussion (*Ref II*, 95–111) affirmed the compatibility and complementarity of the two concepts of the Church, namely *'creatura verbi'*, more identified with the Reformed, and *'sacramentum gratiae'*, more identified with the Catholic understanding of the Church. Now in fact they can be seen as "expressing the same instrumental reality under different aspects, as complementary to each other or as two sides of the same coin. They can become the poles of a creative tension between our churches" (*Ref II*, 113; cf. *Ref III, 190*). On the basis of an exploration of the patristic literature the dialogue was able to conclude: "We can now affirm, in light of our investigation both of the kingdom and of the patristic literature, not only that these visions are mutually informative and complementary but also that neither is fully adequate without the other. A 'sacramental' church that does not give proper place to the Word of God would be essentially incomplete; a church that is truly a creation of the Word will celebrate that Word liturgically and sacramentally. If our churches differ according to these two visions, perhaps it is less because either church is convinced that the church is only *creatura verbi* or only *sacramentum gratiae* and more because each tradition has emphasized one aspect to the point of de-emphasizing or neglecting the other" (*Ref III*, 193).

While Lutherans note affinities regarding the new Catholic understanding of the church as 'sacrament' , they are nevertheless reticent about the description of the Church as 'sacrament' which they are concerned may blur the distinction between Jesus Christ Himself as the "single sacrament of God" and the Church as the recipient of salvation (cf. L–C *Church and Justification*, 128). But dialogue on this topic did lead to affirming that "[t]here is agreement among Lutherans and Catholics that the church is instrument and sign of salvation and, in this sense, 'sacrament' of salvation" (L–C *Church and Justification*, 134; cf. 131–133). The Lutheran–Catholic dialogue refers to the WCC Mission Conference in Melbourne in 1980, whose message it cites as its own: "The good news of the kingdom must be presented to the world by the church, the body of Christ, the sacrament of the kingdom in every place and time" (L–C *Church and Justification*, 305).

According to ARCIC, "The Church as *koinonia* requires visible expression because it is intended to be the 'sacrament' of God's saving work" (ARCIC *FR Introduction*, 7). "To speak of the Church as sacrament is to affirm that in and through the communion of all those who confess Jesus Christ and who live according to their confession, God realizes his plan of salvation for all the world" (ARCIC *Church*, 22; cf. *Salvation*, 29). "The Church is both the sign of salvation in Christ, for to be saved is to be brought into communion with God through Him, and at the same time the instrument of salvation, as the community through which this salvation is offered and received. This is what is meant when the Church is described as an 'effective sign', given by God in the face of human sinfulness, division and alienation" (ARCIC *Church,* 19).

The Methodist–Catholic dialogue has increasingly used sacramental language of the Church. The Singapore Report (1991) notes, "At Vatican II the Roman Catholic Church referred to the Church in terms of a 'sacrament of salvation' (*Ad gentes,* 5; cf. *Lumen gentium,* 1). Methodists would prefer the word 'sign' to sacrament, but the meaning in each case is essentially the same, because the Church obeys the mandate of its Founder to preach to all nations the Gospel of salvation it has received" (M–C *Singapore,* 91). The Seoul Report (2006) summarizes its discussion on sacramentality by citing and making its own the Final Report of the 1985 Extraordinary Synod's affirmation that "The Church as communion is a sacrament for the salvation of the world" (Final Report II D 1); (M–C *Seoul,* 103; cf. *Nairobi,* 9; *Rio,* 96). The Methodist–Catholic dialogue also refers to the Church as empowered to serve as "a sign, sacrament and harbinger of the Kingdom of God in the time between the times" (M–C *Nairobi,* 8). In the Seoul Report, Methodists and Catholics recognise that "the grace of salvation is present and effective" in each other's Christian communities (M–C *Seoul,* 144).

The use of sacramental language in all four dialogues and its compatibility and complementarity with the original Reformation view of the Church as *creatura verbi* can be seen as an important ecumenical breakthrough; this achievement of the dialogues provides a solid common basis and can have far-reaching consequences for the further dialogues – a result confirmed by the increasingly common understanding of the Church as communion.

3. Church as Communion/Koinonia

36. In all four dialogues the biblical and patristic understanding of the Church as communion/*koinonia* progressively emerged as a fundamental concept for describing the Church.[18] Already the Second Vatican Council had laid the basis for an eucharistic communio-ecclesiology (*LG* 3 and 7); the Extraordinary Synod of Bishops in 1985 declared *communio* as the Council's key concept. According to the Council the Church is constituted as communion in accordance with the highest exemplar and source of the communion in the Trinity (cf. *LG* 4; *UR* 2).

a) Communion in the ARCIC documents

37. The language of communion has emerged especially in the Anglican–Catholic dialogue. "Fundamental to all our Statements is the concept of koinonia (communion) ... it is the term that most aptly expresses the mystery underlying the various New Testament images of the Church" (ARCIC *FR Introduction*, 4). The Final Report of 1981 sees *koinonia* with each other in the Church as an expression of our communion with God in Jesus Christ, through the power of the Holy Spirit (cf. ARCIC *FR Introduction,* 5), and therefore the expression of *koinonia* in the Church is a sign that God's purpose in Christ is being fulfilled. "The Church as koinonia requires visible expression because it is intended to be the 'sacrament' of God's saving work" (ARCIC *FR Introduction,* 7). This makes the search for unity between Catholics and Anglicans an imperative: "Those who have received the same word of God and have been baptized in the same Spirit cannot, without disobedience, acquiesce in a state of separation" (ARCIC *FR Introduction,* 9).

The 1976 statement *Authority in the Church I* provides detail about how *koinonia* is structured and served, noting that it is the bishop who "is responsible for preserving and promoting the integrity of the *koinonia*" (ARCIC *Authority I*, 5). The document adds that a genuine exercise of primacy "will foster the koinonia by helping the bishops in their task of apostolic leadership both in their local church and in the Church universal" (ARCIC *Authority I*, 21).

38. Subsequently, the notion of communion was developed in ARCIC's second phase, most notably in the 1991 Agreed Statement *Church as Communion*. The document explains that its purpose "is to give substance to the affirmation that Anglicans and Roman Catholics are already in a real though as yet imperfect communion and to enable us to recognize the degree of communion that exists both within and between us" (ARCIC *Church*, 2). This suggests that the argument outlined by the commission can be weighed to assess how close the Anglican Communion and the Catholic Church are to reaching a common understanding of the Church as *koinonia*. The Statement explores the consequences of describing the Church as communion: "Communion implies that the Church is a dynamic reality moving towards its fulfilment. ... [T]his focus on communion enables us to affirm that which is already realized in the Church, the eucharistic community" (ARCIC *Church*, 3). However, "to understand the Church in terms of communion confronts Christians with the scandal of our divisions. Christian disunity obscures God's invitation to communion for all humankind and makes the Gospel we proclaim harder to hear" (ARCIC *Church*, 4).

Communion with God in Christ is continually renewed by the Spirit, and so the Church is itself a visible and effective sign, and an instrument of salvation (cf. ARCIC *Church*, 17). This sacramental nature of the Church is "especially manifest in the common celebration of the eucharist" (ARCIC *Church*, 24).

The Statement underlines the relationship between communion and apostolicity. Diverse expressions of the one Gospel "must remain faithful to the tradition received from the apostles" (ARCIC *Church,* 29). "Whenever ... Christians are no longer able to receive and pass on the truth within the one community of faith, communion is impoverished" (ARCIC *Church*, 30). "Thus the apostolic tradition is fundamental to the Church's communion which spans time and space" (ARCIC *Church,* 31).

The Statement also considers the elements necessary for ecclesial communion. "For all the local churches to be together in communion ... it is required that all the essential constitutive elements of ecclesial communion are present and mutually recognized in each of them" (ARCIC *Church,* 43). Ecclesial communion requires "the confession of the one apostolic faith, revealed in the Scriptures, and set forth in the Creeds. It is founded upon one baptism. The one celebration of the eucharist is its pre-eminent expression and focus. It necessarily finds expression in shared commitment to the mission entrusted by Christ to his Church ... Also constitutive of life in communion is acceptance of the same basic moral values" (ARCIC *Church*, 45) The episcopate has an especial responsibility to nurture communion, and "[i]n the context of the communion of all the churches the episcopal ministry of a universal primate finds its role as the visible focus of unity" (ARCIC *Church,* 45).

39. The 1999 Agreed Statement *The Gift of Authority* develops the consensus on authority in the Church within the understanding of a communion ecclesiology. The document

emphasises that the local church should always be seen in the context of the indispensable communion of all the churches. Tradition is the means by which "the Holy Spirit forms, maintains and sustains the communion of the local churches from one generation to the next. The handing on and reception of apostolic Tradition is an act of communion whereby the Spirit unites the local churches of our day with those that preceded them in the one apostolic faith" (ARCIC *Gift*, 16). Consequently, communion in the apostolic tradition has two dimensions: diachronic ("the transmission of the Gospel from one generation to another") and synchronic ("the communion of the churches in all places in that one Gospel") (cf. ARCIC *Gift*, 26). Fidelity in communion by local churches is termed 'synodality' or 'walking together' (cf. ARCIC *Gift*, 34). The bishop is a key agent in this (cf. ARCIC *Gift*, 36), so that "[b]y their sensus fidei the faithful are able in conscience both to recognise God at work in the bishop's exercise of authority, and also to respond to it as believers" (ARCIC *Gift*, 36). Synodality means that "[n]o local church that participates in the living Tradition can regard itself as self-sufficient" (ARCIC *Gift*, 37)

The Statement *Church as Communion* concludes with a positive assessment of shared conviction between Anglicans and Catholics about communion, which "enables them to recognize in each other's churches a true affinity" (ARCIC *Church*, 49). While separation has led inevitably to separate cultural traditions, "these developments when held in complementarity can contribute to a fuller understanding of communion" (ARCIC *Church*, 53). The Commission concludes that, despite obstacles, "our two Communions agree in their understanding of the Church as communion" (ARCIC *Church*, 56). The Statement *The Gift of Authority* also concludes that Anglicans and Catholics need to give greater visible expression to their already existing communion: "Anglican and Roman Catholic bishops should find ways of cooperating and developing relationships of mutual accountability in their exercise of oversight. At this new stage we have not only to do together whatever we can, but also to be together all that our existing koinonia allows" (ARCIC *Gift*, 58).

But it is notable that although the notion of *koinonia* has been influential in Anglican ecclesiology, recent developments are causing Anglicans to give renewed attention to their structures of communion (cf. IARCCUM *GTUM*, 21). This may indicate a need to reassess ARCIC's claim that "our two communions agree in their understanding of the Church as communion" (ARCIC *Church*, 56). For immediately after this affirmation the Statement notes that the ordination of women in some Anglican provinces will, citing the words of Pope John Paul II, "effectively block the path to the mutual recognition of ministries" (ARCIC *Church*, 57) (see section below on ordained ministry).

b) *Communion in the other dialogues*

40. The concept of Church as communion became increasingly central also in the other dialogues. According to the Lutheran–Catholic dialogue, "Participation in the communion of the three divine persons is constitutive for the being and life of the church as expressed in the three New Testament descriptions of it as 'people of God', 'body of Christ', and 'temple of the Holy Spirit'. Thus the church also shares in the communion of the Father with the Son and of both with the Holy Spirit. The unity of the church as communion of the faithful has its roots in the trinitarian communion itself, as this is expressed in the greeting of the first letter of John: '. . . so that you also may have fellowship with us; and truly our fellowship is with the Father and with

his Son Jesus Christ' (1 John 1:3; cf. John 17:21)" (L–C *Church and Justification*, 63; cf. 64 and 65).[19]

According to the Reformed–Catholic dialogue, "Sharing word and sacrament in the presence of the Triune God, the church discovers anew its own nature as a communion and becomes what it is: the people of God, the body of Christ and the temple of the Holy Spirit (cf. Eph 2:21)" (*Ref III*, 165; cf. *Ref I*, 73). Furthermore, there are profound links between communion and the Kingdom of God. "By seeking greater visible communion, against all the stumbling blocks which stand in the way, Christians strive to respond more fully to God's will for the complete realization of the kingdom" (*Ref III*, 164; cf. 19).

The Methodist–Catholic dialogue partners presented *Towards a Statement on the Church* to the World Methodist Council meeting in Nairobi in 1986. The document bases its vision on the concept of *koinonia*. "Because God so loved the world, he sent his Son and the Holy Spirit to draw us into communion with himself. This sharing in God's life, which resulted from the mission of the Son and the Holy Spirit, found expression in a visible *koinonia* of Christ's disciples, the Church" (M–C *Nairobi*, 1; cf. *Seoul*, 51) The dialogue partners see *koinonia* as an apt term to express unity within diversity. "This [term] implies that within the one Church in which there is basic agreement in faith, doctrine, and structure essential for mission, there is room for various 'ecclesial traditions', each characterized by a particular style of theology, worship, spirituality and discipline" (M–C *Nairobi*, 24). Yet "[t]here have to be limits to variety; some arise from the need to promote cohesion and cooperation, but the basic structures of the Church also set limits that exclude whatever would disrupt communion in faith, order and sacramental life" (M–C *Nairobi*, 28).

The Statement *The Grace Given You in Christ* (2006) aims to use the notion of an *'exchange of gifts'* to deepen mutual understanding and recognition. Catholics and Methodists determine "to return to the concrete reality of one another, to look one another in the eye, and with love and esteem to acknowledge what we truly see to be of Christ and of the Gospel, and thereby of the Church, in one another" (M–C *Seoul*, 97). Already, the basic but radical shift from historical attitudes that this represents has made it possible to see the way forward in formerly intractable problems, such as the interconnectional nature of the Church, structures of authority, sacraments and visible structures (cf. M–C *Seoul*, 99–106).

Thus *communio* is not only a key concept to describe the nature of the Church as modelled on the image of the Trinitarian *communio*, but also a key concept for the life of the Church as communion between ordained ministry and lay people, men and women, and their exchange of gifts; for the process of consensus- and reception-building; and not least for ecumenical communication among the churches and church communities and their exchange of gifts. This will assist in overcoming contradictory positions by achieving unity within diversity of complementary positions.

B. SOURCE OF AUTHORITY IN THE CHURCH

1. *Primary Authority of Jesus Christ*

41. The Church has no other authority than the authority she received from hearing the Gospel of Jesus Christ witnessed once for all by the apostles. Just as the Church is the body of Christ, and the ministry of the Church continues the mission

and ministry of Christ, the authority of the Church derives ultimately from Jesus Christ.

In this sense the question of Christ's authority in the Church was present in the Lutheran–Catholic dialogue from its very beginning (cf. L–C *Malta*, 14–17) and was later taken up in its second phase which addressed ministry in the Church. Lutherans and Catholics stated together, "Inasmuch as the ministry is exercised on behalf of Jesus Christ and makes him present, it has authority over against the community. 'He who hears you hears me' (Lk 10:16)" (L–C *Ministry*, 23). In a similar way the Reformed–Catholic dialogue has stated, "We are agreed that the Church has its authority to the extent that it listens to the Word Christ speaks to it ever afresh" (*Ref I*, 24). "Christ is 'the Shepherd and Guardian (episkopos)' of all souls (1 Pet 2.25)" (*Ref II*, 135).

In offering summary quotes from ARCIC, *GTUM* presents an overview of Anglican–Catholic insight into this topic that reflects all the dialogues. "Anglicans and Roman Catholics agree that the primary authority for all Christians is Jesus Christ himself. 'To him God has given all authority in heaven and on earth' (citing ARCIC *Authority I*, 1). To follow Christ is to be set under the authority of Christ. The authority of the Church is derived from and wholly dependent upon the authority of Christ (cf. Matthew 11.27, 28.18ff.). 'This is Christian authority: when Christians so act and speak, men perceive the authoritative word of Christ' (citing *Authority I*, 3). 'It is in conformity with the mind and example of Christ that the Church is called to exercise authority (cf. Luke 22.24–27; John 13.14–15; Philippians 2.1–11)' (citing ARCIC *Gift*, 5). His authority 'was demonstrated by his self–giving service in sacrificial love (cf. Mark 10.45)' (citing *Gift*, 9)" (IARCCUM *GTUM*, 62).

According to the Methodist–Catholic dialogue, "The Eternal Logos, through the incarnation, brought God's final revelation to humankind and became the redeemer of the world and the Lord of the Church. The Eternal Word made flesh is the ultimate norm of all the Church's life and doctrine, orienting all that is done and taught in the Church toward the praise and worship of God the Father, by the grace and power of the Holy Spirit" (M–C *Brighton*, 16). Methodists and Catholics affirm their "common acceptance of the paramount authority of Christ in His Church" (M-C *Denver,* 102).

— 2. *Apostolicity of the Church*

a) *The whole Church on the foundation of the Apostles*

42. In the Lutheran–Catholic dialogue the normative nature of the apostolic origin was already dealt with in the first phase of the dialogue (cf. L–C *Malta*, 51-53). In the third phase Catholics and Lutherans affirm together: "The church stands once for all on the foundations of the apostles .... The post-apostolic church must forever maintain its relation to its apostolic beginning" (L–C *Ministry,* 16). "The Holy Spirit unites the Church, lastingly and ever anew, with Jesus Christ and with its apostolic foundation. By the power and guidance of the Holy Spirit, the Church is equipped for its mission in manifold but ever–present ways" (L–C *Apostolicity,* 10). Furthermore, the Lutheran–Catholic dialogue states, "The church is apostolic on the basis of the apostolic gospel and in its faithfulness to it. This gospel is continually prior to the church, as Paul says, 'God was ... entrusting the message of reconciliation to us. So we are ambassadors for Christ, since God is making his appeal through us; we entreat you on behalf of Christ, be reconciled to God' (2 Cor 5:19c–20). The

apostles who were called to be witnesses of the Risen Jesus Christ are the first and normative witnesses of the gospel. In the characteristic of being eye–witnesses they have no successors, but their testimony remains foundational for the church of all times. The Church can be apostolic solely by agreeing with the witness of the apostles" (L–C *Apostolicity*, 271; cf. *Church and Justification*, 44–47; *Apostolicity*, 147–148 and 150).

The Reformed–Catholic dialogue describes the apostolicity of the Church as follows: "The whole Church is apostolic. To be an apostle means to be sent, to have a particular mission. The notion of mission is essential for understanding the ministry of the Church. As Christ is sent by the Father, so the Church is sent by Christ. But this mission of the Church has not simply a Christological reference. The sending of Christ and the equipment of the Church in his service are also works of the Holy Spirit. The mission of the Holy Spirit belongs to the constitution of the Church and her ministry, not merely to their effective functioning. Too often, imbalances in theologies of the ministry are the result and sign of an insufficiently trinitarian theology. It is by the power of the Spirit that the Lord sustains his people in their apostolic vocation. This power manifests itself in a variety of ways which are charismata – gracious gifts of the one Spirit (cf. 1 Cor 12:4ff). Guided by and instrumental to the work of God in this world, the Church has a charismatic character" (*Ref I*, 94). "The Church is apostolic", observes the dialogue, "because it lives the faith of the original apostles, continues the mission given by Christ to them, and remains in the service and way of life testified to by those apostles. The canonical scriptures are the normative expression of this apostolicity. It is within the normative expression of this apostolicity contained in the New Testament that a witness is given to the special ministry given by Christ to the Twelve, and to Peter within that circle of Twelve" (*Ref I*, 95).

According to ARCIC, "In the early church the apostles exercised a ministry which remains of fundamental significance for the Church of all ages. It is difficult to deduce, from the New Testament use of 'apostle' for the Twelve, Paul and others, a precise portrait of an apostle, but two primary features of the original apostolate are clearly discernible: a special relationship with the historical Christ, and a commission from him to the Church and the world (Matt 28:10; Mark 3:14). All Christian apostolate originates in the sending of the Son by the Father. The Church is apostolic not only because its faith and life must reflect the witness to Jesus Christ given in the early Church by the apostles, but also because it is charged to continue in the apostles' commission to communicate to the world what it has received. Within the whole history of mankind the Church is to be the community of reconciliation" (ARCIC *Ministry*, 4). Furthermore, "The person and work of Jesus Christ, preached by the apostles and set forth and interpreted in the New Testament writings, through the inspiration of the Holy Spirit, are the primary norm for Christian faith and life" (ARCIC *Authority I Elucidation*, 2).

The Methodist–Catholic dialogue affirms, "Unity in faith, mission and sacramental life can be achieved only on an apostolic basis. As the Dublin report already recognized, 'We all agree that the Church's apostolicity involves continuous faithfulness in doctrine, ministry, sacrament and life to the teaching of the New Testament' " (M–C *Nairobi*, 31 citing *Dublin*, 84).

b) Succession in apostolic ministry

43. The dialogues also address the question of how the authority of the apostles becomes present in the Church, i.e., apostolic succession, both in the broader meaning of the term and specifically in relation to ministry. At this point, one of the main sources of division and one of the most debated and most difficult questions of the ecumenical dialogue is encountered.[20]

ARCIC texts show that Anglican and Catholic positions are close. "Each local church is rooted in the witness of the apostles and entrusted with the apostolic mission" (ARCIC *Authority I*, 8). "We both maintain that *episcope* must be exercised by ministers ordained in the apostolic succession (cf. §16)" (ARCIC *Ministry Elucidation*, 4). ARCIC's understanding of apostolic succession is set forth in the context of discussing episcopal ordination: "In the ordination of a new bishop, other bishops lay hands on him, as they request the gift of the Spirit for his ministry and receive him into their ministerial fellowship. Because they are entrusted with the oversight of other churches, this participation in his ordination signifies that this new bishop and his church are within the communion of churches. Moreover, because they are representative of their churches in fidelity to the teaching and mission of the apostles and are members of the episcopal college, their participation also ensures the historical continuity of this church with the apostolic Church and of its bishop with the original apostolic ministry. The communion of the churches in mission, faith, and holiness, through time and space, is thus symbolized and maintained in the bishop. Here are comprised the essential features of what is meant in our two traditions by ordination in the apostolic succession" (ARCIC *Ministry*, 16; cf. *FR Introduction*, 7).

The Lutheran–Catholic dialogue distinguishes between apostolic succession in faith (apostolic succession in a substantive sense) and apostolic succession as ministerial succession of bishops (cf. L–C *Ministry*, 59). Then it affirms, "As regards the succession of ministries, the joint starting point for both Catholics and Lutherans is that there is an integral relation between the witness of the gospel and witnesses to the gospel. The witness to the gospel has been entrusted to the church as a whole. Therefore, the whole church as the *ecclesia apostolica* stands in the apostolic succession. Succession in the sense of the succession of ministers must be seen within the succession of the whole church in the apostolic faith" (*Ministry*, 61; cf. *Malta*, 48). Lutherans can accept the historic succession as a sign of unity, which is "meaningful not as isolated act, but only as it contributes to the unity of the church in faith and witnesses to the universality of the gospel" (*Ministry*, 66).

In the fourth phase the Lutheran-Catholic dialogue reaffirmed this position. "Thus fidelity to the apostolic gospel has priority in the interplay of *traditio, successio* and *communio*" (L–C *Apostolicity*, 291). Then with reference to the agreement in the fundamental truths of the doctrine of justification it goes a noticeable step further and states a differentiated consensus: "But if the consensus of bishops is the definitive sign of apostolicity of their doctrine, then Catholics cannot exclude these other *episkopoi* from the circle of those whose consensus is according to the Catholic view the sign of apostolicity of doctrine" (L–C *Apostolicity*, 291).[21]

The Reformed–Catholic dialogue does not go so far. It also describes "several senses of 'apostolic succession'; but when the phrase is taken in its usual meaning to refer to the continuity of the special ministry, it is clear that it occurs within the apostolicity which belongs to the whole church. Reformed and Roman Catholics both believe that there is an apostolic succession essential to the life of the Church, though we locate that succession differently" (*Ref I*, 100). "Apostolic succession", the dialogue goes on to say, "consists at least in continuity of apostolic doctrine; but this is not in opposition to succession through continuity of ordained ministry. The continuity of right doctrine is guarded by the application of Holy Scripture and transmitted by the continuity of the teaching function of the special ministry. As with all aspects of the Church's ministry, so with the particular case of apostolic succession: it requires at once a historical continuity with the original apostles and a contemporary and graciously renewed action of the Holy Spirit" (*Ref I*, 101).

The dialogue is clear about the remaining differences. "The Reformed churches give first consideration to continuity in the confession of faith and in the teaching of Gospel doctrine. It is in this sense that the Church remains apostolic and the ministers raised up in it by the Spirit form part of the apostolic succession. The Catholic Church, for its part, considers that this apostolicity of faith and preaching as well as that of the administration of the sacraments are linked to a certain number of visible signs through which the Spirit works, in particular to the apostolic succession of bishops" (*Ref II*, 120).

"Methodists and Catholics agree that the ministry of the apostles was essential to the proclamation and spread of the good news during the first century. It is clear from the New Testament that different functions and offices were also recognized early in the Church as gifts from God, 'to equip the saints for the work of ministry, for building up the body of Christ' (Eph 4:12). Scholars find the historical record diverse, noting that episcopacy as an office developed gradually in a variety of places. Roman Catholic teaching emphasizes that there is nevertheless a collegial succession from the apostles to the bishops. There is agreement between Catholics and Methodists that the ministry of *episcope* (oversight) was always exercised in the Church: 'From apostolic times, certain ordained persons have been entrusted with the particular tasks of superintendency' (*The Book of Discipline of the United Methodist Church* [1996], 401)" (M–C *Brighton*, 71). Methodists and Catholics nonetheless "differ in the account we give of the apostolic succession" (M–C *Nairobi* 31; cf. M-C *Rio* 129–30).

The Methodist-Catholic dialogue noted a number of differences concerning apostolic ministry between Methodists and Roman Catholics. "The crucial examples are the threefold ministry and the apostolic succession. Methodists are not in principle opposed to the ministry's being in the threefold form or in the historical succession. But they do not consider either of these to be necessary for the church or for the ministry" (M–C *Dublin*, 104).

c)   Issues to be resolved

44. While there is a fundamental agreement on apostolicity and apostolic succession between Anglicans and Catholics, ARCIC's agreed statements acknowledge also that the Catholic Church has not recognised Anglican Orders (cf. ARCIC *FR Introduction*, 9; *Ministry*, 17). The official position is still that of the Letter of Leo XIII *Apostolicae Curae* (1896) which ruled against the validity of Anglican Orders. But *Ministry* 17 argued that the agreement reached on essential matters pertaining to ministry now puts the question of the recognition of Anglican Orders in a new context, inviting a reappraisal of *Apostolicae Curae*. Full recognition presupposes full agreement on the sacramental character of ordination.

More recent developments, however, especially the ordination of women to the priesthood and increasingly to the episcopacy in many Anglican provinces, have hindered further constructive discussion of this suggestion (see section below on ordained ministry).

In the other dialogues the differences are of more fundamental character, and are linked with continuing different positions on church ministries (see below). Among them the Lutheran–Catholic dialogue is the most advanced; it states a fundamental mutual recognition of ecclesial apostolicity, but identifies also the respective differences in doctrine and church life. "A first limitation rests on differences in understanding ordination to the pastorate, ministry in apostolic succession, and the office of bishop in the church. Second, while we agree on Sacred Scripture being the norm of all preaching, teaching, and Christian life, we differ on how Scripture is to be authentically interpreted and how the teaching office serves Scripture in the latter's guidance of the church's teaching and practice" (L–C *Apostolicity,* 162).

From these thorny questions emerge deeper fundamental problems, most notably the sacramental understanding of the Church and her ministries. Though there is an emerging consensus on a sacramental understanding of the Church, this recent development still needs to be reflected on and applied to the concrete questions of ministry and apostolic succession. This problem will be recalled in the concluding reflections of this chapter.

3. *Scripture and Tradition*

45. The relation between Scripture and Tradition is one of the classic controversial themes between the ecclesial commu-

nities stemming from the Reformation and the Catholic Church. In recent times the discussion was placed in a broader context and viewed within a new hermeneutical horizon. This new situation has emerged for several reasons that relate to a new understanding of Tradition and its relationship to Scripture.[22] The changed circumstances are also echoed in the Dogmatic Constitution on divine revelation *Dei verbum* (DV 7–10), which laid down the fundamental outlines for revisiting the old controversial positions.

a) *Beyond old conflicts: interrelation between Scripture and Tradition*

46. In the Lutheran-Catholic dialogue[23] the new hermeneutical context was present from the start. "From the very beginning, the gospel of Jesus Christ was the subject matter of the tradition. Out of and in the service of the proclamation of the gospel, certain writings were composed which were later designated as the New Testament. This poses the old controversial question regarding the relationship of Scripture and tradition in a new way. The Scripture can no longer be exclusively contrasted with tradition, because the New Testament itself is the product of primitive tradition" (L–C *Malta,* 17). Instead of isolating the principle of *sola scriptura,* the scriptures were seen in the context of the living word of preaching of the gospel: "Yet as the witness to the fundamental tradition, Scripture has a normative role for the entire later tradition of the church" (L–C *Malta,* 17; cf. *Unity,* 57; *Ways,* 64).

Lutherans and Catholics, after exploring the relationship of Scripture and Tradition (cf. L–C *Apostolicity,* 442–447), have now reached the point of saying, "Therefore regarding Scripture and tradition, Lutherans and Catholics are in such an extensive agreement that their different emphases do not of themselves require maintaining the present division of the churches. In this area, there is unity in reconciled diversity" (L–C *Apostolicity,* 448; cf. *Unity*, 54). Nevertheless it remains true that "[w]hile Scripture and tradition are connected, Scripture should not be absorbed into the tradition process, but should remain permanently superior as a critical norm, coming from the apostolic origins, which is superior to the traditions of the church" (L–C *Apostolicity*, 447).

According to the Reformed–Catholic dialogue, "Norms for the belief and practice of the Church are not simply to be found in isolated proof-texts or in clearly discernible primitive patterns, but in the New Testament considered as a whole and as testimony to the divine purpose and mission for Israel, for the Church and for all humanity" (*Ref I,* 15). Then it adds, "In the history of the Church, the difference between Catholics and Reformed has always focused on the alternative: 'Scripture and Tradition' and 'Scripture only'. Catholics stressed the need for and the authority of the Church's teaching office in the interpretation of Scripture, whereas the Reformed declared that Scripture interprets itself and, as God's Word, must be strictly distinguished from all human tradition, desiring in this way to do justice not only to the doctrine of justification but also to the total witness of the Old and New Testaments" (*Ref I*, 24). "Both on the Catholic and on the Reformed side today, the problem is no longer presented in terms of the battle lines of post-Tridentine polemic" *(Ref I,* 25).

The Anglican–Catholic dialogue does not directly address the historical conflict regarding the relationship between Scripture and Tradition, but has stated, "We exist as Christians by the Tradition of the Gospel, testified in Scripture, transmitted in and by the Church through the power of the Holy Spirit.

'Within Tradition the Scriptures occupy a unique and normative place and belong to what has been given once for all' " (IARCCUM *GTUM,* 29 citing ARCIC *Gift,* 19). It speaks of "the dynamic interdependence of Scripture and apostolic Tradition and the normative place of Scripture within Tradition" (ARCIC *Gift,* 52). "At a very early stage, by the guidance of the Holy Spirit, 'the Church was led to acknowledge the canon of Scripture as both test and norm' in order to safeguard the authenticity of its memory (citing *Church,* 26). Therefore the Scriptures as the uniquely inspired witness to divine revelation have a unique role in keeping alive the Church's memory of the teaching and work of Christ. We agree that the Church's teaching, preaching and action must constantly be measured against the Scriptures" (IARCCUM *GTUM,* 29).

According to ARCIC, "Through the gift of the Spirit the apostolic community came to recognize in the words and deeds of Jesus the saving activity of God and their mission to proclaim to all men the good news of salvation. Therefore they preached Jesus through whom God has spoken finally to men. Assisted by the Holy Spirit they transmitted what they had heard and seen of the life and words of Jesus and their interpretation of his redemptive work. Consequently the inspired documents in which this is related came to be accepted by the Church as a normative record of the authentic foundation of the faith" (ARCIC *Authority I,* 2; cf. *Authority I Elucidation,* 2). "To these [Scriptures] the Church has recourse for the inspiration of its life and mission; to these the Church refers its teaching and practice. Through these written words the authority of the Word of God is conveyed. Entrusted with these documents, the Christian community is enabled by the Holy Spirit to live out the Gospel and so to be led into all truth" (ARCIC *Authority I,* 2).

Methodists and Catholics affirm, "The old oppositions of Scripture and Tradition have given way to an understanding which we share, that Scripture in witness to the living tradition from which it arose has a normative role for the total tradition of the Church as it lives and is guided still by the Spirit of truth" (M–C *Honolulu,* 34). "[T]he search for ecumenical reconciliation has revealed only too clearly the difficulty of reuniting Scripture and Tradition once they have been notionally separated. Scripture was written within Tradition, yet Scripture is normative for Tradition. The one is only intelligible in terms of the other" (M–C *Singapore,* 21). The Methodist–Catholic dialogue affirms, "In proclamation and instruction the written Word in the Scriptures has primacy over all later formulations of divine revelation. It provides a permanent standard of belief . . ." (M–C *Brighton*, 17).

Methodists and Catholics have reflected, "The Word is present in Tradition as the communication of the Gospel to new generations of believers. Tradition is 'the history of that continuing environment of grace in and by which all Christians live', it finds its 'focal expression' in Scripture (citing *The Book of Disciple of the United Methodist Church* [1996], §77), and it will always be faithful to the biblical message. Since they preserve the proclamation of the news of salvation by the prophets and apostles, the Scriptures are at the same time the model and the heart of the Tradition. In this Tradition, by which the Word is transmitted from age to age, the Word is read, proclaimed, explained and celebrated. The Tradition acquires normative value as its fidelity to the biblical norm and to the Eternal Word is recognized. 'Scripture was written within Tradition, yet Scripture is normative for Tradition. The one is only intelligible in terms of the other' (citing *Singapore,* 21). That there is a harmony between Scripture, Tradition, and the Christian life of faith and worship is part of the self-understanding of the Church and integral to the manner in which the Church, in the Holy Spirit, transmits itself from generation to generation. There is a growing convergence between Methodists and Catholics on what Pope John Paul II has called 'the relationship between Sacred Scripture, as the highest authority in matters of faith, and Sacred Tradition, as indispensable to the interpretation of the Word of God' (citing *Ut unum sint,* 79)" (M–C *Brighton,* 18).

b) *The Word of God as common source of Scripture and Tradition*

47. While the 'Word of God' is sometimes used synonymously with the Scriptures, it is also used in relation to what God has revealed in Jesus Christ, and as such is understood as a common source of Scripture and Tradition. The dialogues show an emerging agreement on this perspective.

Participants in the Lutheran–Catholic dialogue agree that "the authority of the church can only be service of the word and that it is not master of the word of the Lord. Therefore the church's tradition must remain open to the word and must transmit it in such a way that the word constantly bestows the understanding which comes from faith and freedom for Christian action" (L–C *Malta,* 21; cf. *Apostolicity,* 410).

The Reformed–Catholic dialogue states, "Since the Second Vatican Council, Catholic teaching has stressed the very close connection between Scripture and Tradition: 'springing from the same divine source, both so to speak coalesce and press towards the same goal' (*Dei verbum,* 9). Scripture and Tradition thus constitute 'the one holy treasure of the Word of God bequeathed to the Church' (*Dei verbum,* 10) with a special dignity attaching to the Scriptures because in them apostolic preaching has been given especially clear expression (cf. *Dei verbum,* 8). In the light of these facts, the customary distinction between Scripture and Tradition as two different sources which operate as norms either alternatively or in parallel has become impossible" (*Ref I,* 25). "We are agreed that as *creatura Verbi* the Church together with its Tradition stands under the living Word of God" (*Ref I,* 26).

Anglicans and Catholics have reflected, "The Word who became flesh and dwelt among us is at the centre of what was transmitted from the beginning and what will be transmitted until the end ... It is the living Word of God, together with the Spirit, who communicates God's invitation to communion to the whole world in every age. Therefore, we rejoice to reaffirm that the Church's mission is most truly that of the Son and the Spirit. Properly understood, tradition is itself an act of communion whereby the Spirit unites the local churches of our day with those that preceded them in the one apostolic faith. The communion of the Church spans time and space" (IARCCUM *GTUM,* 27).

In this context ARCIC and the Methodist–Catholic dialogues speak more explicitly of Tradition as the transmission of the Gospel through time. ARCIC reflected, "The revealed Word, to which the apostolic community originally bore witness, is received and communicated through the life of the whole Christian community. Tradition (*paradosis*) refers to this process. The Gospel of Christ crucified and risen is continually handed on and received (cf. 1 Cor 15.3) in the Christian churches. This tradition, or handing on, of the Gospel is the work of the Spirit, especially through the ministry of Word and Sacrament and in the common life of the people of God. Tradition is a dynamic process, communicating to each generation what was delivered once for all to the apostolic community. ... In the economy (*oikonomia*) of

God's love for humanity, the Word who became flesh and dwelt among us is at the centre of what was transmitted from the beginning and what will be transmitted until the end. . . . Apostolic Tradition is a gift of God which must be constantly received anew. By means of it, the Holy Spirit forms, maintains and sustains the communion of the local churches from one generation to the next. The handing on and reception of apostolic Tradition is an act of communion whereby the Spirit unites the local churches of our day with those that preceded them in the one apostolic faith. The process of tradition entails the constant and perpetual reception and communication of the revealed Word of God in many varied circumstances and continually changing times" (ARCIC *Gift,* 14 and 16; cf. IARCCUM *GTUM,* 64).

Similarly the Methodist–Catholic dialogue states, "The apostolic mission, the charge laid on the apostles to transmit the message of Jesus Christ to their own and to all successive generations, is precisely the service of the Word. The person of Christ, his teaching and his work for us: it was to all this that the apostles bore witness, for all this is God's Word" (11). . . . "A profound understanding of the Church must begin with a reflection on the Word of God, who brings the Church into being and continues to make the Church what it is. The Word spoken to us in Christ calls forth our response. Thus, the Church is sustained by a conversation, initiated by the Lord" (13). . . . "In order to fulfil this saving purpose, he called into being the Church where the Word's recreating power is evident, remaking people into a community that could share his life and live in harmonious relationships with one another. Thus the Church is the place where the Word of God is spoken, heard, responded to, and confessed (*Rom* 10:8–17)" (15). . . . "The Tradition received by the apostles itself continues an unbroken process of communication between God and human beings. ... The written word of Scripture is its permanent norm" (16). (M–C *Singapore*, 11, 13, 15, 16; cf. also *Brighton*, 16–18).

c) *The New Testament as product of the living Tradition of the Gospel*

48. "Catholics and Lutherans agree, not only that Scripture developed historically from a process of tradition both in Israel and the apostolic church, but as well that Scripture is oriented toward a process of being interpreted in the context of ecclesial tradition" (L–C *Apostolicity*, 442). The New Testament conveys the living Tradition of the Gospel. "The Scriptures were accepted by the ancient Church because these writings attested the living tradition of the Gospel (summed up in the so-called *regula fidei*) because they were written by the apostles as eyewitnesses or by their disciples, handed down by the Church which itself has an apostolic origin. In accordance with both the Catholic and the Reformed tradition, the Church played its part in the process whereby the canon was formed, even if we cannot define this part more precisely" (*Ref I*, 32).

According to ARCIC, "Through the gift of the Spirit the apostolic community came to recognize in the words and deeds of Jesus the saving activity of God and their mission to proclaim to all men the good news of salvation. Therefore they preached Jesus through whom God has spoken finally to men. Assisted by the Holy Spirit they transmitted what they had heard and seen of the life and words of Jesus and their interpretation of his redemptive work. Consequently the inspired documents in which this is related came to be accepted by the Church as a normative record of the authentic foundation of the faith" (ARCIC *Authority I*, 2; cf. *Gift*, 19). "The content of the faith is the truth of Christ

Jesus as it has been transmitted through the apostles. This God-given deposit of faith cannot be dissociated from the gift of the Holy Spirit. Central to the mission of the Spirit is the safeguarding and quickening of the memory of the teaching and work of Christ and of his exaltation, of which the apostolic community was the first witness. To safeguard the authenticity of its memory the Church was led to acknowledge the canon of Scripture as both test and norm" (ARCIC *Church,* 26).

According to the Methodist–Catholic dialogue, the fullness of divine revelation is found in Jesus Christ, and "[t]he first response to this revelation in Christ is formulated in the Scriptures of the New Testament" (M–C *Rio,* 6).

What can be said of the New Testament is true also of the Canon of Scriptures as a whole. "It is the conviction of both churches that God's word is also transmitted through church traditions even though they differ in their theological evaluations. The canon of Holy Scripture is certainly itself a weighty and fundamental part of church tradition" (L–C *Ways,* 64; cf. *Apostolicity,* 390–410). "Historical researches have shown not only how the New Testament writings are themselves already the outcome of and witness to traditions, but also how the canonization of the New Testament was part of the development of tradition" (*Ref I,* 25). "In accordance with both the Catholic and the Reformed tradition, the Church played its part in the process whereby the canon was formed, even if we cannot define this part more precisely. In the light of this common understanding, the traditional controversy as to whether canonization was the decision of a 'possessing' Church or the receiving recognition of an 'obeying' Church is out of date" (*Ref I,* 32).

"The formation of the canon of the Scriptures was an integral part of the process of tradition. The Church's recognition of these Scriptures as canonical, after a long period of critical discernment, was at the same time an act of obedience and of authority. It was an act of obedience in that the Church discerned and received God's life-giving 'Yes' through the Scriptures, accepting them as the norm of faith. It was an act of authority in that the Church, under the guidance of the Holy Spirit, received and handed on these texts, declaring that they were inspired and that others were not to be included in the canon" (ARCIC *Gift*, 22).

The Methodist–Catholic dialogue alludes to this theme in a more general way in the context of speaking about the evolution of the threefold ministry. "It is acknowledged that it [the threefold ministry] became generally established in the second and third centuries and was clearly universal in the same post-New Testament period in which the Scriptural canon was established and the classical creeds were formed. Roman Catholics and some Methodists would see a similarity in these three developments under the guidance of the Holy Spirit" (M–C *Honolulu*, 29).

d) The importance of the early Councils of the Church

49. Related to the question of Tradition is the question of the importance and authority of the early councils of the Church. In this regard The Anglican–Catholic dialogue notes, "In both our traditions the appeal to Scripture, to the creeds, to the Fathers and to the definitions of the councils of the early Church is regarded as basic and normative" (ARCIC *Authority I*, 18). "Both Communions agree that, under the guidance of the Holy Spirit, the Tradition of the Gospel is alive in the Church, in continuity with the earliest Christian centuries when the apostolic witness, memory and inter-

pretation took normative form in the canon of Scripture, and the first four councils formulated fundamental and binding doctrines of Christian faith" (IARCCUM *GTUM,* 32). After registering significant agreement IARCCUM's *GTUM* noted, "Anglicans and Roman Catholics diverge with regard to the status both of the councils held, and of the doctrines formulated, in the intervening centuries up to today. There are further divergences in the way in which teaching authority in the life of the Church is exercised and the authentic tradition is discerned" (IARCCUM *GTUM,* 32; cf. 71 and 73–76). "Anglicans historically have only recognised the binding authority of the first four ecumenical councils. While they affirm some of the content of successive councils, they believe that only those decisions which can be demonstrated from Scripture are binding on the faithful" (IARCCUM *GTUM,* 69).

Lutherans and Catholics state, "At the great councils, deliberations took place before an open book of the Gospels, placed on a chair to indicate that Christ was presiding. But while later theological writers defended conciliar teaching by amassing Scripture texts in expounding doctrines, councils themselves judged controverted doctrines by their agreement or disagreement with the teaching of earlier councils and works of recognized orthodox teachers. When synodical letters communicated the decisions of councils, as after Ephesus in 431, the basis given was the 'faith of Nicaea' taken as the epitome of biblical doctrine" (L–C *Apostolicity,* 340; cf. 323–326; 336–341).

Reformed and Catholics, affirming their common confession of faith in Jesus Christ, the only mediator between God and humankind, have stated, "[W]e recognize together in the teaching of the ancient church, the force of a *norma normata*, i.e., an authority which is subject to the authority of the scripture, and we desire to maintain that teaching in its purity. The teaching of the church ought to be an authentic explanation of the Trinitarian and Christological affirmations of the early confessions of faith and the early councils" (*Ref II*, 67). Furthermore, the Reformed in expressing their difficulties with the notion of ecclesiastical infallibility say that their "misgivings ... do not detract from the decisive though subordinate weight given in the Reformed tradition to the ancient Ecumenical Councils in the transmission and interpretation of the Gospel" (*Ref I*, 42).

"Both the Roman Catholic Church and the Methodist Churches hold that the first Ecumenical Councils defined a fundamental, genuine and valid formulation and interpretation of the Apostolic Faith" (M–C *Rio*, 68; cf. *Brighton*, 22 and *Seoul*, 21). Some of the dialogues even express openness, albeit if in nuanced ways, to the authority of later councils. The Methodist–Catholic dialogue would add, "Properly understood the decisions of the ecumenical councils which met in the first centuries command assent throughout the whole Church, and there is no reason to think that at the end of the patristic era God stopped enabling his Church to speak in such a way. Other occasions have called, and may still call for such authoritative guidance" (M–C *Nairobi*, 65).

C. The Ministry in the Church

1. The Mission and Ministry of the Whole People of God

50. Ministry in the Church is one of the most discussed and – despite many new insights and convergences – one of the enduring controversial issues in ecumenical dialogue. Today,

there is a common starting point in affirming the continuation of the mission and ministry of Jesus Christ in the mission and ministry of the whole people of God. Thus, according to the Lutheran–Catholic dialogue, "Just as Christ, in the Holy Spirit, was sent into the world by the Father, he now sends his disciples into the world so that in his name they bring the Gospel to all humankind (Matt 28:19, Mark 16:15). The promise and the outpouring of the Holy Spirit assures the apostles that they act on behalf of the risen Christ, and not by their own strength" (L–C *Ministry,* 10; cf. *Malta,* 49).[24]

"Catholics and Lutherans are in agreement that all the baptized who believe in Christ share in the priesthood of Christ and are thus commissioned to 'proclaim the mighty acts of him who called you out of darkness into his marvellous light' (1 Pet 2:9). Hence no member lacks a part to play in the mission of the whole body" (L–C *Apostolicity,* 273).

According to the Reformed–Catholic dialogue, "The Church bases its life on the sending of Christ into the world and the sending of the Holy Spirit that men and women may be joined to Christ in his service; its authority is inseparable from its service in the world which is the object of God's creative and reconciling love. As servants of their servant Lord, ministers of the Church must serve the world with wisdom and patience. Without lively personal discipleship, there can be no credible exercise of office. At the same time, those who bear office in the Church must adhere to the promise that the Lord determines to build up his community even through imperfect servants. Our common effort at a deeper common understanding of the nature of ministry in the Church has also to be motivated by concern for the service of the Church in the world" (*Ref I,* 93).

Because the whole Church is apostolic, one can speak of the ministry of the whole Church. "The extension of Christ's ministry, including his priestly office, belongs to all members of his body (cf. 1 Petr 2:5–9). Each member contributes to that total ministry in a different fashion; there is a distribution of diverse gifts (cf. 1 Cor 12:4–11), and every baptized believer exercises his or her share in the total priesthood differently. This calling to the priesthood of all those who share in the body of Christ by baptism does not mean that there are no particular functions which are proper to the special ministry within the body of Christ" (*Ref I,* 96).

According to ARCIC, "The life and self-offering of Christ perfectly express what it is to serve God and man. All Christian ministry, whose purpose is always to build up the community (*koinonia*), flows and takes its shape from this source and model. The communion of men with God (and with each other) requires their reconciliation. This reconciliation, accomplished by the death and resurrection of Jesus Christ, is being realized in the life of the Church through the response of faith. While the Church is still in process of sanctification, its mission is nevertheless to be the instrument by which this reconciliation in Christ is proclaimed, his love manifested, and the means of salvation offered to men" (ARCIC *Ministry,* 3).

ARCIC affirms that "the priesthood of the whole people of God (1 Peter 2:5) is the consequence of incorporation by baptism into Christ. This priesthood of all the faithful (§7) is not a matter of disagreement between us" (ARCIC *Ministry Elucidation*, 2). "The Christian community exists to give glory to God through the fulfilment of the Father's purpose. All Christians are called to serve this purpose by their life of prayer and surrender to divine grace, and by their careful attention to the needs of all human beings. They should witness to God's compassion for all mankind and his concern for justice in the affairs of men. They should offer themselves to God in praise and worship, and devote their energies to bringing men into the fellowship of Christ's people, and so under his rule of love" (ARCIC *Ministry*, 7).

For the Methodist–Catholic dialogue, "The fundamental ministry is Christ's own ministry, whose goal is to reconcile all people to God and to each other and to bring them into a new community in which they can grow together to their full freedom as children of God. This ministry was focused in Christ's life and death and resurrection. It did not end with his life on earth, but by the power of the Spirit continues now in and through his church. Christ still chooses and equips people for his ministry, just as he did in the beginning" (M–C *Dublin*, 77). "The whole people of God has been sent by Christ into the world to witness to the love of the Father in the power of the Holy Spirit. In this sense it is apostolic. All its members are gifted by the Spirit, and there is no gift without its corresponding service" (M–C *Rio*, 84). "All those to whom the apostles transmit their faith have a share in their work. All are called to witness. All are called to glorify God and intercede for the world. All are called to serve their neighbour" (M–C *Rio*, 87; cf. *Dublin*, 81).

2. Ordained Ministry

2.1 THE ARCIC CONSENSUS ON ORDAINED MINISTRY

51. On ordained ministry and its relationship to the ministry of the whole Church, ARCIC has a prominent role because its treatment of ministry has been submitted to the respective authorities and has been given a positive evaluation. ARCIC's principal work on ministry is found in three documents: the

1973 agreed statement *Ministry and Ordination*; the 1979 *Ministry Elucidation*, which sought to address questions or critiques arising from a first round of responses to the text; and the 1994 *Clarifications* prepared by an ARCIC I sub-commission in order to address concerns raised in the official Catholic response, and later endorsed by the members of ARCIC II.[25]

a) *The ordained ministry: an integral element of the Church*
52. ARCIC expressed confidence that "the ordained ministry is an essential element of the Church" *(Clarifications)* and that already in the New Testament, "we can see elements which will remain at the heart of what today we call ordination" (ARCIC *Ministry* 5). "The New Testament shows that ministerial office played an essential part in the life of the Church in the first century, and we believe that the provision of a ministry of this kind is part of God's design for his people. Normative principles governing the purpose and function of the ministry are already present in the New Testament documents (e.g. Mk 10:43-45; Acts 20:28; 1 Tim 4:12-16; 1 Pet 5:1-4)" (ARCIC *Ministry,* 6; cf. *Ministry Elucidation,* 4).

Clarifications developed this historical reflection further, stating: "After the resurrection the Holy Spirit conferred upon the apostolic group what was necessary for the accomplishment of their commission. They in turn were led by the Lord to choose collaborators and successors who, through the laying on of hands, were endowed with the same gift of God for ministry in the Church. Thus the sacramental ministry is something positively intended by God and derives from the will and institution of Jesus Christ."

ARCIC stresses that Christian ministers are at once members of the Church and those who, "particularly in presiding at the eucharist – [are] representative of the whole Church in the fulfilment of its priestly vocation of self-offering to God as a living sacrifice (Rom 12:1)" (ARCIC *Ministry,* 13). "Just as the original apostles did not choose themselves but were chosen and commissioned by Jesus, so those who are ordained are called by Christ in the Church and through the Church. Not only is their vocation from Christ but their qualification for exercising such a ministry is the gift of the Spirit ..." (ARCIC *Ministry,* 14).

According to ARCIC, "The ordained ministry can only be rightly understood within [the] broader context of various ministries, all of which are the work of one and the same Spirit" (ARCIC *Ministry,* 2). While *Ministry* 7 notes that the "goal of the ordained ministry is to serve this priesthood of all the faithful", *Ministry Elucidation* expands on it as follows: "In common Christian usage the term priesthood is employed in three distinct ways: the priesthood of Christ, the priesthood of the people of God, the priesthood of the ordained ministry.... The word priesthood is used by way of analogy when it is applied to the people of God and to the ordained ministry. These are two distinct realities which relate, each in its own way, to the high priesthood of Christ, the unique priesthood of the new covenant, which is their source and model. These considerations ... indicate the significance of the statement that the ordained ministry 'is not an extension of the common Christian priesthood but belongs to another realm of the gifts of the Spirit'" (ARCIC *Ministry Elucidation,* 2 citing *Ministry,* 13).

b) *Ordination: sacrament and sacramental ministry*
53. Anglicans and Catholics agree on the sacramental nature of ordination. "In this sacramental act, the gift of God is bestowed upon the ministers, with the promise of divine

grace for their work and for their sanctification; the ministry of Christ is presented to them as a model for their own; and the Spirit seals those whom he has chosen and consecrated. Just as Christ has united the Church inseparably with himself, and as God calls all the faithful to life-long discipleship, so the gifts and calling of God to the ministers are irrevocable. For this reason, ordination is unrepeatable in both our churches" (ARCIC *Ministry*, 15; cf. *Ministry Elucidation*, 3).

Ordination involves an invocation of the Holy Spirit and a laying on of hands. "Not only is their vocation from Christ but their qualification for exercising such a ministry is the gift of the Spirit: 'our sufficiency is from God, who has qualified us to be ministers of a new covenant, not in a written code but in the Spirit' (2 Cor 3:5-6). This is expressed in ordination, when the bishop prays God to grant the gift of the Holy Spirit and lays hands on the candidate as the outward sign of the gifts bestowed. Because ministry is in and for the community and because ordination is an act in which the whole Church of God is involved, this prayer and laying on of hands takes place within the context of the eucharist" (ARCIC *Ministry*, 14).

Before giving specific attention to the presidency of the Eucharist, ARCIC addresses sacramental ministry in a more general way. "The part of the ministers in the celebration of the sacraments is one with their responsibility for ministry of the word. In both word and sacrament Christians meet the living Word of God. The responsibility of the ministers in the Christian community involves them in being not only the persons who normally administer baptism, but also those who admit converts to the communion of the faithful and restore those who have fallen away. Authority to pronounce God's forgiveness of sin, given to bishops and presbyters at their ordination, is exercised by them to bring Christians to a closer communion with God and with their fellow men through Christ and to assure them of God's continuing love and mercy" (ARCIC *Ministry,* 11).

Given that the Eucharist is the central act of Christian worship, which "nourishes the Church's life for the fulfilment of its mission", Anglicans and Catholics are in agreement that "he who has oversight in his church and is the focus of its unity should preside at the celebration of the eucharist" (ARCIC *Ministry,* 12). It is within the celebration of the Eucharist that the essential priestly nature of Christian ministry is most clearly seen. "[O]rdained ministry is called priestly principally because it has a particular sacramental relationship with Christ as High Priest" (ARCIC *Ministry Elucidation,* 2). "The priestly sacrifice of Jesus was unique, as is also his continuing High Priesthood. Despite the fact that in the New Testament ministers are never called 'priests' (*hiereis*), Christians came to see the priestly role of Christ reflected in these ministers and used priestly terms in describing them. Because the eucharist is the memorial of the sacrifice of Christ, the action of the presiding minister in reciting again the words of Christ at the last supper and distributing to the assembly the holy gifts is seen to stand in a sacramental relation to what Christ himself did in offering his own sacrifice. So our two traditions commonly use priestly terms in speaking about the ordained ministry. . .. There is in the eucharist a memorial (*anamnesis*) [cf. *Eucharistic Doctrine*, 5] of the totality of God's reconciling action in Christ, who through this minister presides at the Lord's Supper and gives himself sacramentally. So it is because the eucharist is central in the Church's life that the essential nature of the Christian ministry, however this may be expressed, is most clearly seen in its celebration. . .." (ARCIC *Ministry,* 13; cf. *Ministry Elucidation* 2; *Clarifications*).

c) *The threefold ministry in the apostolic succession*

54. After pointing to a variety of New Testament images which give shape to ordained ministry in the Church (cf. ARCIC *Ministry,* 8), ARCIC focuses its attention on responsibility for 'oversight' (*episcopé*), which is an "essential element in the ordained ministry.. ... This responsibility involves fidelity to the apostolic faith, its embodiment in the life of the Church today, and its transmission to the Church of tomorrow. Presbyters are joined with the bishop in his oversight of the church and in the ministry of the word and the sacraments; they are given authority to preside at the eucharist and to pronounce absolution. Deacons, although not so empowered, are associated with bishops and presbyters in the ministry of word and sacrament, and assist in oversight" (ARCIC *Ministry,* 9). Anglicans and Catholics are in agreement that "*episcope* must be exercised by ministers ordained in the apostolic succession. Both our communions have retained and remained faithful to the threefold ministry centred on episcopacy as the form in which this *episcope* is to be exercised" (ARCIC *Ministry Elucidation,* 4; cf. *Ministry,* 16). "Both presbyters and deacons are ordained by the bishop" (ARCIC *Ministry,* 16).[26]

The threefold order of ministry emerged already in early periods of the Church. "Just as the formation of the canon of the New Testament was a process incomplete until the second half of the second century, so also the full emergence of the threefold ministry of bishop, presbyter, and deacon required a longer period than the apostolic age. Thereafter this threefold structure became universal in the Church" (ARCIC *Ministry,* 6). ARCIC's *Ministry Elucidation* 4 expanded on this, noting that "[e]arly in the second century, the pattern of a threefold ministry centered on episcopacy was already discernible, and probably widely found (cf. the Epistles of Ignatius to the Ephesians, 4; Magnesians, 13;

Trallians, 2; Philadelphians, 2; Smyrnaeans, 8). It was recognized that such ministry must be in continuity not only with the apostolic faith but also with the commission given to the apostles (cf. the First Epistle of Clement, 42)."

d) *Remaining issues*

55. The official response process allows us to speak of an ARCIC consensus on ministry, a consensus needing to be qualified in two ways. Firstly, when ARCIC *Ministry* 1 spoke of "the consensus we have reached", it added, "This statement is not designed to be an exhaustive treatment of ministry. It seeks to express our basic agreement in the doctrinal areas that have been the source of controversy between us, in the wider context of our common convictions about the ministry." The text's conclusion spoke of a consensus "on questions where agreement is indispensable for unity" (ARCIC *Ministry,* 17). Secondly, the consensus acknowledged that it concerned the *nature* of ordained ministry, not the question of who can or cannot be ordained. Given this, ARCIC has always been clear that the agreement achieved so far cannot be the only factor in permitting a reappraisal of Anglican Orders (cf. ARCIC *Ministry,* 17).

This was reflected in the official Catholic response to the *Final Report*, which stated that "the question of the subject of ordination is linked with the nature of the sacrament of Holy Orders. Differences in this connection must therefore affect the agreement reached on Ministry and Ordination." In calling for further dialogue in this regard, *Clarifications* noted: "We are confronted with an issue that involves far more than the question of ministry as such. It raises profound questions of ecclesiology and authority in relation to Tradition".

Addressing questions relating to Anglican orders and the ordination of women, IARCCUM's *GTUM* reflected, "In his Apostolic Letter on Anglican Orders, *Apostolicae Curae* (1896), Pope Leo XIII ruled against the validity of Anglican Orders. The question of validity remains a fundamental obstacle to the recognition of Anglican ministries by the Catholic Church. In the light of the agreements on the Eucharist and ministry set out both in the ARCIC statements and in the official responses of both Communions, there is evidence that we have a common intention in ordination and in the celebration of the Eucharist. This awareness would have to be part of any fresh evaluation of Anglican Orders" (IARCCUM *GTUM,* 60).

Unfortunately, subsequent developments have prevented further constructive discussion of this suggestion and, as *Church as Communion* 57 pointed out, have effectively blocked the path to the mutual recognition of ministries. Between the publication of *Ministry* in 1973 and the *Ministry Elucidation* in 1979, the decision of certain Anglican Provinces to proceed with the ordination of women to the priesthood and the episcopacy emerged as a new complicating factor from the perspective of the Catholic Church. The *Elucidation* cited a letter of Pope Paul VI to Archbishop of Canterbury Donald Coggan commenting that this had created "a new and grave obstacle to the reconciliation of our communions", but noted ARCIC's conviction "that the principles upon which its doctrinal agreement rests are not affected by such ordinations; for it was concerned with the origin and nature of the ordained ministry and not with the question who can or cannot be ordained" (ARCIC *Ministry Elucidation,* 5, citing Letter of Pope Paul VI to Archbishop Donald Coggan, 23 March 1976, AAS 68). (Cf. also Letter of Pope John Paul II to the Archbishop of Canterbury, 8th December 1988; IARC-CUM *GTUM* 45,60).

A growing number of Anglican provinces, after reflection and debate, and despite sometimes strong differences of opinion within those provinces, have proceeded to ordain women to the presbyterate and to the episcopate. While they have acted "in the conviction that there are no theological objections to such a development, and that they are not departing from the traditional understanding of apostolic ministry or the nature of ministry as set forth in the ARCIC statements" (IARCCUM *GTUM,* 61), Pope John Paul II expressed the conviction that "the Church has no authority whatsoever to confer priestly ordination on women" (*Ordinatio Sacerdotalis,* 1994, 4).

2.2 THE ORDAINED MINISTRY ACCORDING TO THE OTHER DIALOGUES

a)   *The ordained ministry: an integral element of the Church*

56.   In the Lutheran-Catholic dialogue the question of the ministry in the Church was present from its beginning (cf. L–C *Malta,* 47-58) and was taken up in the second phase of the dialogue (cf. L–C *Ministry,* 16 ff). The ministry "signifies the priority of divine initiative and authority in the Church's existence" (L–C *Ministry,* 20 citing *Accra* 14). The ministry in the Church is, therefore, subordinated to the one ministry of Jesus Christ. "Consequently, this ministry is not simply a delegation 'from below', but is instituted by Jesus Christ" (L–C *Ministry,* 20). "It is Jesus Christ who, in the Holy Spirit, is acting in the preaching of the Word of God, in the administration of the sacraments, and in the pastoral service. Jesus Christ, acting in the present, takes the minister into his service; the minister is only his tool and instrument. Jesus Christ is the one and only high priest of the New Covenant" (L–C *Ministry,* 21; cf. *Apostolicity,* 274).

The one ministry of Jesus Christ is exercised with a view to building up the community. For Lutherans and Catholics it is fundamental to a proper understanding of the ministerial office that "the office of the ministry stands over against the community as well as within the community" (L–C *Malta*, 50; cf. *Ministry*, 23). "Inasmuch as the ministry is exercised on behalf of Jesus Christ and makes him present, it has authority over against the community. 'He who hears you hears me' (Lk 10:16). The authority of the ministry must therefore not be understood as delegated by the community" (L–C *Ministry*, 23; cf. 24).

In the fourth phase the dialogue returned again to this issue. The dialogue stated, "The ordained ministry belongs to the essential elements which, through the power of the Holy Spirit, contribute to the church being and remaining apostolic, while they in turn express the church's apostolicity. To fulfil that task, the ministry itself must be ministry in apostolic succession" (L–C *Apostolicity*, 270). "For both Catholics and Lutherans, the common priesthood of all the baptized and the special, ordained ministry do not compete with each other. Instead, the special ministry is precisely service to the common priesthood of all. . . . As service to the word of God this ministry stands over against the congregation, while at the same time the minister also belongs to the congregation" (*Apostolicity*, 275). "Catholics and Lutherans affirm together that God instituted the ministry and that it is necessary for the being of the church" (*Apostolicity*, 276).

The Reformed–Catholic dialogue states, "Ordination, or setting apart for the exercise of these special services, takes place within the context of the believing community. Hence consultation with that community, profession of faith before that community, and liturgical participation by that community belong to the process of ordination. This is important to underline because we need to go beyond an understanding of ordination which suggests that those consecrated to the special ministry are given a potestas and derive a dignity from Christ without reference to the believing community" (*Ref I*, 97). Reformed and Catholics affirm, "The continuity of this special ministry of Word and Sacrament is integral to that dimension of Christ's sovereign and gracious presence which is mediated through the Church. The forgiveness of sins and call to repentance are the exercise of the power of the keys in the upbuilding of the Church. This power Christ entrusted to the apostles with the assurance of his continued presence to the end of the age. The apostolic continuity depends not only on Christ's original commission but also on his continual call and action" (*Ref I*, 99).

In a similar line the Methodist–Catholic dialogue states, "The ordained minister, although his task may be different from that of others, does not work in isolation, but in cooperation with other ministries given to the church. Indeed all members of the church by their Christian vocation have a gift from God of ministry" (M–C *Dublin*, 80). "The ordained ministry is given to the church by God, and the apostles were the first 'ministers of the gospel'. They were commissioned by Christ himself, and each ordained minister in his turn receives through the church at his ordination the commission of Christ. Thus this ministry has existed from New Testament times until now" (M–C *Dublin*, 82). "Roman Catholics and Methodists agree that by ordination a new and permanent relationship with Christ and his church is established. The ordained minister is called and enabled by the Holy Spirit to be the representative person who focuses in his ministry the manifold ministries of the whole church" (M–C *Dublin*, 98; cf. *Singapore*, 71).

According to the Methodist–Catholic dialogue, within the ministry of the whole people of God, "there has been, from the beginning, a ministry uniquely called and empowered to build up the body of Christ in love. This is 'apostolic' in the specific sense because it began with Christ's choosing from among his disciples, the twelve 'whom he named apostles' (*Lk* 6:13). It has continued through the ages in those who follow them in that ministry" (M–C *Rio*, 84).

b) *Constitutive elements of ordination*

57. "Various Catholic–Lutheran dialogues on the ordained ministry in the church have shown that, even though Lutherans do not speak of ordination as a sacrament, there is yet substantial convergence between the Catholic and the Lutheran understanding and practice wherever ordination is celebrated through the laying-on of hands and prayer (epiclesis) as an act of blessing, and wherever it is taught 'that through the act of ordination the Holy Spirit gives grace strengthening the ordained person for the lifetime ministry of word and sacrament'. Lutheran tradition has taken account of this even though it does not include ordination among the sacraments in the strict sense. 'In principle ... [it does] not reject' the sacramental understanding of ordination" (L–C *Unity*, 78 citing *Ministry*, 33; cf. *Apostolicity*, 277).

"Our churches are thus able today to declare in common that the essential and specific function of the ordained minister is to assemble and build up the Christian community by proclaiming the word of God, celebrating the sacraments and presiding over the liturgical, missionary and diaconal life of the community" (L–C *Ministry*, 31; cf. *Malta*, 47–67; *Ways*, 21–70; *Christ*, 16; *Apostolicity*, 274).

In the Reformed–Catholic dialogue we read, "The liturgical validation at the time of the act of ordination includes the invocation of the Holy Spirit ('epiclesis') with the laying on of hands by other ordained ministers. The invocation of the Holy Spirit is a reminder of the essential role which the doctrine of the Trinity must fulfil in any balanced understanding of the ministry. It gives proper weight both to Jesus Christ's historical and present action and to the continual operation of the Holy Spirit. The laying on of hands is an efficacious sign which initiates and confirms the believer in the ministry conferred. It is not the community which produces and authorizes the office but the living Christ who bestows it on the community and incorporates this office into its life" (*Ref I,* 98).

"Within apostolicity in general there is a special ministry to which the administration of Word and Sacrament is entrusted. That special ministry is one of the charismata for the exercise of particular services within the whole body" (*Ref I,* 97).

The dialogue with the Methodists agreed that constitutive elements of ordination include an *epiclesis* or invocation of the Holy Spirit and the *laying on of hands*. According to the Methodist–Catholic dialogue, "Both our traditions retain the practice, attested in the New Testament documents, of setting apart for ministry by the laying on of hands with prayer; prayer is made for the gift of the Holy Spirit appropriate to the particular form of ministry. Ordination takes place in an assembly of the Church in which the people give their assent to the candidates, appropriate scriptures are read, and candidates profess their adherence to the faith of the Church. Through the laying on of hands ordinands are incorporated into the existing body of ministers" (M–C *Singapore,* 80).

"Chosen from among the people, the ordained ministers represent the people before God as they bring together the prayers of the community. Entrusted with the pastoral care of the community, they act in Christ's name and person as they lead the people in prayer, proclaim and explain the Word, and administer the sacraments of faith" (M–C *Singapore,* 71). "They transmit what they have received: the good news as taught from apostolic times, the sacraments as signs and instruments of the Lord's saving presence and action, the call to holiness that the Holy Spirit addresses to all" (M–C *Singapore,* 72; cf. 60–61).

c) The emergence of the threefold ministry

58. In the Lutheran–Catholic dialogue the historical emergence of church structures and of the threefold ministry was already an issue in its first phase (cf. L–C *Malta*, 54 f). The question was taken up in the second phase, which noted a high degree of agreement that this development of the one apostolic ministry into a more local and more regional ministry has taken place with the help of the Holy Spirit, and to this degree constitutes something essential for the church (cf. L–C *Ministry*, 49).

In the fourth phase this issue was treated in detail (cf. L–C *Apostolicity*, 46–49; 172–193). Both partners stated: "The Early Church's structure of the threefold ministry is not attested as such in the New Testament, but it did emerge by the further development of offices referred to in the New Testament which were then brought together into a particular configuration. The development of the office of ministry in the Early Church is a specific form of the reception of New Testament testimony to ministries and charisms which were effective in the church of the apostles" (*Apostolicity*, 169). For Catholics the development of the threefold ministry has to be understood as the irreversible formation of a basic structure, which belongs to the fullness of the nature of the Church (cf. *Apostolicity*, 281), whereas Lutherans in the sixteenth century were "faced with a choice between fidelity to the gospel and submission to bishops, which constrained them to give precedence to the former over the latter. Precisely because they held ministerial office to be essential for the existence of the Church, they had to practice presbyterial ordination ... It is almost universally the practice in Lutheran churches today that the responsibility for ordaining pastors is assigned to persons who hold supra-local-office" (*Apostolicity*, 282). Though differences remain, the document concludes: "Therefore the issue is both the possibility of a differentiated consensus on the doctrine of ministry and an approach to the differing forms of ministry, in which one discovers so much ground that reciprocal recognition of ministries would be possible" (*Apostolicity*, 292). This is a far-reaching thesis, which has still to be discussed (cf. above footnote 21).

The Reformed–Catholic dialogue acknowledges, "Leadership in the New Testament took different forms at various times and places under diverse names (see e.g., Acts 1.20–25; 20.17; 28; 1 Cor 12.28; Eph 4.11–13; Phil 1.1; 1 Tim 3.1–13; 4.14; 5.3–22; Tit 1.5–9). ... From the various forms of leadership mentioned in the Pastorals there emerged a pattern of episcopoi, presbyters and deacons, which became established by the end of the second century" (*Ref II*, 136). "This pattern of leadership developed from some New Testament forms, while other (even earlier) New Testament forms did not develop. The spread and theological interpretation of ecclesial leadership in the immediate post New Testament period must be seen against the background of the wider development of the early church and its articulation of the faith (see 1 Clem 40–44, especially 42, 1–2, 4; 44, 1–2;

Ignatius of Antioch, Eph 2.1–5; Magn 2; Hippolytus, Apost. Trad.). In the course of history some of the functions of such leaders underwent change; even so the ministry of bishops, presbyters and deacons became in the ancient church the universal pattern of church leadership" (*Ref II*, 137).

Methodists and Catholics in dialogue note, "From the written data alone it cannot be ascertained with certainty whether the threefold ministry of bishop, presbyter, deacon, which developed from the New Testament. . . was established in the first century" (M–C *Nairobi*, 29). However, "As time passed, the Church was led by the Spirit to recognize the threefold ministry of bishop, presbyter and deacon as normative; some other patterns of ministry that may be discerned in the New Testament became assimilated to the threefold one" (M–C *Singapore*, 61). "Methodists are not in principle opposed to the ministry's being in the threefold form or in the historical succession. But they do not consider either of these to be necessary for the church or for the minister. (In fact all Methodists preserve a form of ministerial succession and most Methodists have a threefold form of ministry)" (M–C *Dublin*, 104; cf. *Brighton*, 71).

d) *Remaining questions*

59. "What is in dispute between Lutherans and Catholics is neither the differentiation nor the distinction between a more local and a more regional ministry, nor that ordination belongs to the regional ministry. The controversy is instead over what makes a person a rightful holder of a regional ministry and what grounds the power to ordain. At issue is apostolic succession in episcopal office. ... It is Catholic doctrine that the practice and doctrine of apostolic succession in the episcopate is, together with the threefold ministry, part of the complete structure of the Church. This succession is

realized in a corporate manner as bishops are taken into the college of Catholic bishops and thereby have the power to ordain. Therefore it is also Catholic doctrine that in Lutheran churches the sacramental sign of ordination is not fully present because those who ordain do not act in communion with and as member of the Catholic episcopal college. Therefore the Second Vatican Council speaks of a *defectus ordinis* (*UR* 22) in these churches" (L–C *Apostolicity,* 283).[27]

"A further difference is connected with the preceding one. 'For Lutherans the local congregation is church in the full sense, for Catholics it is the local church led by a bishop' " (L–C *Apostolicity,* 284 citing *Church and Justification,* 84). "He is the connecting link between the local, the regional and the universal levels of the church. He holds that function of course only as a member of the college of bishops under the head of this college, the Pope. According to Catholic teaching the legitimacy and the authenticity of the ministry depend on this visible and physical mediation of catholicity. Consequently, ordination by a member of the college of bishops is the efficacious sacramental sign that the office is characterized in its origins by an essential association with the apostolic tradition and the universal church. When Lutherans say that the local church is church in the full sense, they presuppose that the congregation assembled for worship stands in an essential relation to the universal church. This is so because the local church is not the whole church although it is wholly church. This relation to the universal church is not something secondary, subsequently added to the worshipping congregation, but is already always intrinsic to it. So this is not the point at which Lutheran and Catholic conceptions diverge. But they answer differently the question of how this relation with the universal church is mediated personally and institutionally. According to Lutheran understanding, a spiritual reality cannot be without a physical, perceptible dimension, because the Holy Spirit creates and maintains faith and the church by making use of the physical word of proclamation and sacraments as means" (L–C *Apostolicity,* 284–285).

All the dialogues agree that the threefold pattern of ministry emerges early in the history of the Church, but there is no consensus on the permanent binding character of this development and whether such a threefold ministry must also be the obligatory pattern today, or whether a plurality of concrete patterns of ministry is possible. Despite this, there is now a growing common understanding on *episcopé* as an essential ministry in the Church.

3. Convergences towards a Common Understanding of Episcopé

a) Episcopé *as element of the ministry in the Church*

60. Notwithstanding the remaining differences on the binding character of the emergence of the threefold ministry, all the dialogues concur on the importance of *episcopé* in the sense of oversight in the Church. While they do not fully agree on who exercises oversight, there are convergences on a number of other important aspects related to *episcopé*.[28]

All of the dialogues make clear that *episcopé* (oversight) is an essential element of ministry and that it functions in the service of Christ and His Body, the Church. This issue became central especially in the Anglican-Catholic dialogue. ARCIC treats *episcopé* within the context of ordained ministry. "[T]hose exercising *episcope* receive the grace appropriate to their calling and those for whom it is exercised must recognize and accept their God-given authority.... The specific oversight of the ordained ministry is exercised and acknowledged when a minister preaches the Gospel, presides at the eucharist, and seeks as pastor to lead the community truly to discern God's word and its relevance to their lives" (ARCIC *Authority Elucidation*, 5). ARCIC speaks of *episcopé* as being exercised "in the name of Christ" (ARCIC *Ministry Elucidation*, 3; cf. IARCCUM *GTUM*, 62) and at the service of the Church.

The Lutheran–Catholic dialogue states, "As far as the question of the episcopal office is concerned, here again it has to be noted that, in accord with the historic church, the Confessio Augustana specifically affirms its desire to maintain the episcopal structure. The assumption here was that the true proclamation of the gospel is helped and not hindered by this office. The Confessio Augustana affirms a ministry of unity and leadership – set over the local ministers – (CA 28), as essential for the church, therefore, even if the actual form to be given to this ministerial office remains open" (L–C *Christ*, 22). "Also according to *Lutheran understanding*, the individual congregation is essentially related to the church as a whole. There is a need beyond the local congregation for leadership services *(episcopé)* with pastoral responsibility for proclamation, sacraments and church unity. Thus in addition to the office of parish pastor, there is a place for supracongregational ministries in the church" (L–C *Ways*, 23; cf. *Ministry*, 44; *Apostolicity*, 279–280).

The Reformed–Catholic dialogue reflects on ministry, including the ministry of oversight. "This mission which the risen Christ committed to the 'eleven' (Mt 28.16) and from which the church arose, implies that one should distinguish between those who announce the gospel ('you') and those to whom it is proclaimed ('make disciples'). It entails, moreover, a ministry of Word, Sacrament and oversight given by Christ to the church to be carried out by some of its members for the good of all. This triple function of the ministry equips the church for its mission in the world" (*Ref II*, 132).

Likewise, "both Catholics and Methodists recognise the need for effective pastoral ministries of unity and oversight (*episcopé*) within the one Church of Christ" (M–C *Seoul*, 61). "All forms of ministry are communal and collegial. They seek to preserve and strengthen the whole community of faith in truth and love, in worship and in mission" (M–C *Seoul*, 91). "Every formal expression of pastoral authority, whether the teaching office of the bishops or the power of councils, synods and conferences, and every expression of prophetic challenge, is to serve the upbuilding of the whole people of God under the lordship of Christ himself" (M–C *Rio*, 72). "Both Roman Catholics and Methodists believe that *episkope* of the churches is a divinely given function" (M–C *Nairobi*, 34). "Roman Catholics and Methodists agree that *episcope* (pastoral care and oversight) belongs essentially to the ordained ministry. Such *episcope* is exercised in different ways in their churches, but in each case it is carefully ordered with the purpose of the building-up and discipline of the faithful, the training of the young, the maintenance of the unity and peace of the church, and in the planning and direction of mission and evangelism" (M–C *Dublin*, 88).

b) Episcopé *as an instrument of unity*
61. In all the dialogues, *episcopé* is understood as an instrument of unity. Identifying elements which constitute ecclesial communion, ARCIC states, "*[E]piscope* exists only to serve *koinonia*. The ordained minister presiding at the eucharist is a sign of Christ gathering his people and giving them his body

and blood. . . . Through the ministry of word and sacrament the Holy Spirit is given for the building up of the body of Christ. It is the responsibility of those exercising *episcope* . . . to keep the community under the law of Christ in mutual love and in concern for others. . ." (ARCIC *FR Introduction*, 6). "For the nurture and growth of this communion, Christ the Lord has provided a ministry of oversight, the fullness of which is entrusted to the episcopate, which has the responsibility of maintaining and expressing the unity of the churches. By shepherding, teaching and the celebration of the sacraments, especially the eucharist, this ministry holds believers together in the communion of the local church and in the wider communion of all the churches" (ARCIC *Church*, 45; cf. 33, 39; cf. also *Gift*, 30).

Lutherans and Catholics have reflected that they "are, therefore, confronted with the empirical fact that in both churches there are local congregational ministers (priest, pastor) as well as also superordinated regional ministries. These regional ministries have the function of pastoral supervision and of service of unity within a larger area. These functions are connected with the commission to preach, administer the sacraments and lead the congregation, and involve teaching and doctrinal discipline, ordination, super-vision, church order" (L–C *Ministry*, 44). The "under-standing by the Early Church of the episcopal office as a service to the koinonia can stimulate, correct and enlarge the view of Catholics and Lutherans in their endeavours for a commonly exercised episcopé. It becomes particularly clear that episcopé is exercised in concert with the church as a whole in a personal, collegial and communal way. Conse-quently, the exercise of the episcopé cannot be separated from the responsibility of the laity or from 'synodality' or conciliarity" (L–C *Unity*, 112).

The Reformed–Catholic dialogue has affirmed that "the ministry of oversight (episkopé) [is] exercised by church members for the fidelity, unity, harmony, growth and discipline of the wayfaring people of God under Christ, who is 'the Shepherd and Guardian (episkopos)' of all souls (1 Pet 2.25). Various 'gifts', 'services', and 'activities', are inspired by God's Spirit in the church (1 Cor 12.4–6), but all members are called upon to be concerned for that same unity, harmony, and upbuilding of the church" (*Ref II*, 135).

According to the Methodist–Catholic dialogue, "The function of oversight entails on the part of the ministers solicitude for all the churches: they are charged to ensure that the community remain one, that it grow in holiness, that it preserve its catholicity, and that it be faithful to apostolic teaching and to the commission of evangelization given by Christ himself" (M–C *Singapore*, 74).

c) Episcopé *and collegiality*

62. The dialogues agree that *episcopé* has to be exercised in a personal, communal and collegial way. Accordingly, *episcopé* must be characterised by collegiality. Anglicans and Catholics understand collegiality specifically in terms of the episcopate, and state the following: "In both our communions, the bishops meet together collegially, not as individuals but as those who have authority within and for the synodal life of the local churches. Consulting the faithful is an aspect of episcopal oversight. Each bishop is both a voice for the local church and one through whom the local church learns from other churches. When bishops take counsel together they seek both to discern and to articulate the *sensus fidelium* as it is present in the local church and in the wider communion of churches" (ARCIC *Gift*, 38).

The Lutheran–Catholic dialogue states that as a service to the *koinonia*, *episcopé* is exercised in concert with the Church as a whole in a personal, collegial and communal way (cf. L–C *Unity*, 112–116). Furthermore, "Catholics and Lutherans say together that the episcope of ministry must be exercised at two different levels, that is, both locally in the congregation and regionally" (L–C *Apostolicity*, 280).

The Reformed–Catholic dialogue states, "We agree that the basic structure of the Church and its ministry is collegial. When one is consecrated to the special ministry, one accepts the discipline of being introduced into a collegial function which includes being subject to others in the Lord and drawing on the comfort and admonition of fellow ministers. This 'collegiality' is expressed on the Reformed side by the synodical polity, and, on the Roman Catholic side, by the episcopal college, the understanding of which is in process of further development. In the Reformed polity, the synod functions as a corporate episcopacy, exercising oversight of pastors and congregations. We consider it would be worth while to investigate in what ways the diverse functions of the Reformed office of elder could be further developed in a modern form and made fruitful in the life of the Church. We agree that the collegial structure must be expressed in different ways in different times and we have to be sensitive to the pluriformity of charismata. This principle of collegiality is not to be limited to the level of the synods, and in the Roman Catholic Church not to the episcopal college, neither to clergy only, but to be realized at all levels of church life" (*Ref I*, 102).

The Methodist–Catholic dialogue asserts, "All forms of ministry are communal and collegial" (M–C *Brighton*, 81). "Both Methodists and Roman Catholics have a strong sense of the corporate nature of the ministry of oversight. This reflects their common emphasis on the connection or communion of local communities of faith with one another in their Christian life, worship and mission. ... Methodists and Catholics affirm together that true Christian faith and discipleship always involve unity with one another in truth and in love" (M–C *Brighton*, 76).

4. Ministry: Exercised within the Church Local and Universal

a) Local and universal dimensions of the Church

63. All of the dialogues affirm both local and universal dimensions of the Church. They affirm that an authentic local church requires it to be in communion with other local churches. They also affirm the need for structures at local and universal levels to maintain and give visible expression to that communion.[29]

According to the Lutheran–Catholic dialogue, "There is only one church of God. In the New Testament the same word ecclesia signifies both the whole church (e.g. Mt 16:18; Gal 1:13) and the church of a region (e.g. Gal 1:2), the church of a city (e.g. Acts 8:1; 1 Cor 11:18) or of a house (e.g. Rom 16:5). Accordingly, Lutherans and Catholics see the church of God in local, regional and universal terms, but these different ways in which the church becomes a reality must be understood on the basis of the one holy catholic and apostolic church, the una sancta of the Creed" (L–C *Church and Justification*, 80; cf. L-C, *Ministry*, 67-73).

Concerning the Church local and universal, the Reformed–Catholic dialogue states, "[B]oth Roman Catholic and Reformed agreed that the Church Catholic is really represented and exists in the local Church" (*Ref I*, 18). At the same time, "the localness and the catholicity of the Church are to be kept in perspective. It is only by participating in the local community that we share in the life of the universal Church, but the local community without universality (in particular the small basic communities but likewise the local Churches at regional level) runs the risk of becoming a ghetto or of being arbitrarily dominated by individuals" (*Ref I,* 62).

According to ARCIC, "The mutual interdependence of all the churches is integral to the reality of the Church as God wills it to be. No local church that participates in the living Tradition can regard itself as self-sufficient" (ARCIC *Gift,* 37). "[B]y means of the communion among those entrusted with the episcopal ministry, the whole Church is made aware of the perceptions and concerns of the local churches: at the same time the local churches are enabled to maintain their place and particular character within the communion of all the churches" (ARCIC *Church,* 33).

According to the Methodist–Catholic dialogue, "Christian communion is more than the fellowship of the members of the same congregation or the same local community. The Church of God has universal dimensions in regard to both time and space" (M–C *Rio,* 126). "From the first call of Jesus to his Apostles, to be called is to be gathered – into local communities (churches) and into one universal communion (the Church)" (M–C *Seoul,* 60).

b)   *Communion and conciliar structures of the Church*

64.   Each local church represents and realises the one Church of Christ; therefore no local church can isolate herself but exists only in communion with all other local churches. In the larger ecumenical dialogue this idea finds expression in the

principle of Conciliarity and conciliar fellowship, which is echoed also in the four bilateral dialogues.[30]

Lutherans and Catholics had reflected on this issue already in *Ministry* 68 and 72. There, they state that the dialogue between their churches "and, in general, ecumenical efforts for visible unity of the church have shown that the structured form needed for full and binding fellowship between churches can be manifold and variable. It is not limited to the hierarchical dimension of the church, but rather embraces the service of the whole people of God, includes the charisms of all the faithful, and expresses itself in synodal structures and processes. At the same time, fellowship in the ordained ministry forms an essential part of the structured church fellowship" (L–C *Unity,* 92). "Catholics and Lutherans together understand that the communion with God mediated through word and sacrament leads to communion of the faithful among themselves. This takes concrete shape in the communion of the churches: the one holy catholic and apostolic church, the una sancta of the creed, is realized in the communio ecclesiarum as local, regional and universal communion, and so as church fellowship" (L–C *Church and Justification,* 79; cf. 105, 191).

In this regard, the Reformed–Catholic dialogue asks that serious consideration be given to the description of conciliar fellowship expressed by the Assembly of the World Council of Churches, Nairobi (1975): "The one Church is to be envisioned as a conciliar fellowship of local churches which are themselves truly united. In this conciliar fellowship each local church possesses, in communion with the others, the fullness of catholicity, witnesses to the same apostolic faith and therefore recognizes the others as belonging to the same Church of Christ and guided by the same Spirit. As the New Delhi Assembly pointed out, they are bound together because they have received the same baptism and share in the same eucharist; they recognize each other's members and ministries. They are one in their common commitment to confess the gospel of Christ by proclamation and service to the world. To this end, each church aims at maintaining sustained and sustaining relationships with her sister churches, expressed in conciliar gatherings whenever required for the fulfilment of this common calling" (*Ref II*, 161 citing *Breaking Barriers*, Nairobi, 1975).

The Reformed–Catholic dialogue speaks of the need for structures of ministry at all levels. "[O]n the question of how the authority of Christ must be exercised in the church, we are in accord that the structure of the ministry is essentially collegial (compare: PCCW [*Ref* I], 102). We agree on the need for episkopé in the church, on the local level (for pastoral care in each congregation), on the regional level (for the link of congregations among themselves), and on the universal level (for the guidance of the supranational communion of churches). There is disagreement between us about who is regarded as episkopos at these different levels and what is the function or role of the episkopos" (*Ref II*, 142). Concerning the universal level, "[t]he Reformed stress the collegial exercise of episkopé. At the local level the responsibility lies with pastors, elders and/or deacons, with a very important role often played by the church meeting. At regional and national levels it is exercised collectively by synods. The same applies, in principle, to the universal level. The Reformed have never given up hope for a universal council based on the authority of the scriptures. That hope has not yet materialized, though ecumenical world assemblies in our century are an important step towards its fulfilment" (*Ref II*, 142).

According to ARCIC, "Each local church is rooted in the witness of the apostles and entrusted with the apostolic mission. Faithful to the Gospel, celebrating the one eucharist and dedicated to the service of the same Lord, it is the Church of Christ. In spite of diversities each local church recognises its own essential features in the others and its true identity with them" (ARCIC *Authority I*, 8; cf. *FR Introduction*, 6). "A local church cannot be truly faithful to Christ if it does not desire to foster universal communion, the embodiment of that unity for which Christ prayed" (ARCIC *Authority I*, 13). "The mutual interdependence of all the churches is integral to the reality of the Church as God wills it to be. No local church that participates in the living Tradition can regard itself as self-sufficient. ... The ministry of the bishop is crucial, for this ministry serves communion within and among local churches" (ARCIC *Gift*, 37).

ARCIC continues by saying that the communion of bishops "with each other is expressed through the incorporation of each bishop into a college of bishops. Bishops are, both personally and collegially, at the service of communion and are concerned for synodality in all its expressions. These expressions have included a wide variety of organs, instruments and institutions, notably synods or councils, local, provincial, worldwide, ecumenical. The maintenance of communion requires that at every level there is a capacity to take decisions appropriate to that level. When those decisions raise serious questions for the wider communion of churches, synodality must find a wider expression" (ARCIC *Gift*, 37).

Among these four dialogues, ARCIC describes the relationship between local and universal dimensions of the Church by speaking of the relationship between conciliarity and primacy at local (diocesan), regional and universal levels of the Church. "The *koinonia* is realized not only in the local Christian communities, but also in the communion of these communities with one another. The unity of local communities under one bishop constitutes what is commonly meant in our two communions by 'a local church' ... Since each bishop must ensure that the local community is distinctively Christian he has to make it aware of the universal communion of which it is part. The bishop expresses this unity of his church with others ..." (ARCIC *Authority I*, 8).

"Both Methodists and Catholics have an essentially 'connectional' understanding of Christ's call to discipleship, to holiness and to mission, always as God's gift and rooted in our sharing in the invisible *koinonia* that is the life of the Holy Trinity. ... There can be no such thing as private and individualistic Christianity. To be Christian is to be joined together in Christ, to belong to the community gathered around the Risen Lord by the power of the Holy Spirit" (M–C *Seoul,* 60). "This dynamic of connection and communion belongs not only to local disciples gathered together in community, but also to the worldwide community of those local communities united together as one Church, the Body of Christ. The Church of Christ is truly present and effective in some way in all local congregations of the faithful who are gathered together by the preaching of the Gospel and for the celebration of the Eucharist (cf. LG §26). But to be truly ecclesial, each community must be open to communion with other such communities. Individual Christians and their communities are essentially linked together in a web of mutual and interdependent relationships" (M–C *Seoul,* 61).

Methodists and Catholics jointly "acknowledge the importance of a structure which binds together local churches to testify to the global nature of the Gospel and of the Church universal. But we have different perceptions about the nature and the theological weight of those structures" (M–C *Rio*, 128). "Both Methodists and Roman Catholics have a strong sense of the corporate nature of the ministry of oversight. This reflects their common emphasis on the connection or communion of local communities of faith with one another in their Christian life, worship and mission. For each Methodist Church, Conference exercises a form of corporate *episcope*. For Catholics, it is the college of bishops united with the Bishop of Rome that exercises such a corporate *episcope*. The unity of local Catholic communities with one another is constituted and served by their communion with their bishop in a diocese, and the unity of their bishops by communion with the Bishop of Rome (M-C *Brighton*, 76).

c) *Remaining issues*

65. Summarising remaining differences pertaining to authority and ministry, *GTUM* notes, "Anglicans and Roman Catholics share a considerable agreement on authority in the Church, although there are a number of remaining issues, including the binding authority of ecumenical councils, and the infallibility of the teaching office of the Church. Anglicans and Catholics continue to reflect upon the relationship between local and universal in the life of the Church, and in particular: on the place and authority of regional and national structures; on the place and role of the laity at every level of the Church's life, particularly in relation to the councils and synods of the Church; on the relationship between collegial and synodical gatherings; and on the place of reception in discerning the mind of Christ for the Church" (IARCCUM *GTUM,* 73). Furthermore, "The question of whether the Anglican Communion is open to instruments of oversight which would allow decisions to be reached which in certain

circumstances would bind the members of every province is an important and topical one. In turn, it has been asked whether in the Catholic Church enough provision has been made to ensure consultation between the Bishop of Rome and the local churches prior to the making of important decisions affecting either a local church or the whole Church" (IARCCUM *GTUM,* 74).

"The communion of Lutheran churches in a worldwide framework is less developed. The competency of leadership bodies above the level of the individual churches and the binding force of their decisions for these churches is variously regulated and insufficiently clarified. Lutherans have different views with regard to whether there ought to be an institutional exercise of a universal ministry of unity and, in such a case, how such a ministry should be structured. But there is no controversy between Lutherans and Catholics concerning the essential relation between each worshipping congregation and the universal church; nor do we differ over this relation being perceptibly represented and mediated in diverse ways. But there is a dispute about what intensity and what structure this relation to the universal church must have for the worshipping congregations and individual to be in accord with their apostolic mission" (L–C *Apostolicity,* 287; cf. *Ministry* 67-73).

The Methodist–Catholic dialogue notes that "our increasing mutual understanding and our growth in agreement on questions of ministry do not exclude the fact that there are areas of serious divergence which require further exploration and discussion. Central to Methodist teaching on the Church is the role of Christian conference in which lay people alongside ordained ministers authoritatively discern the will of God and the truth of the Gospel. There remain aspects of teaching and ecclesial elements which Catholics regard as essential to what we must hold in common in order to have full communion and to be fully the Church of Christ. These include a precise understanding of the sacramental nature of ordination, the magisterial role of the episcopate in apostolic succession, the assurance asserted of certain authoritative acts of teaching, and the place and role of the Petrine Ministry" (M–C *Seoul*, 92).

— 5. *Universal primacy/Petrine ministry*

66. All the dialogues deal with the question of a universal ministry of unity, revealing several approaches to a Petrine ministry, especially in the biblical discussion of the role of Peter in the New Testament. In each of the four dialogues there has been at least initial reflection on doctrinal questions related to the Petrine ministry, such as the need for *episcopé* at the universal level; in some there has even been a cautious/ qualified openness to the specific idea of a Petrine ministry; three of the dialogues directly mention the Bishop of Rome as the one who holds the Petrine ministry and would hold it in a united Church of the future; and at least in one dialogue, the Catholic Church's dialogue partner expresses a willingness to receive aspects of the Petrine ministry into its life even now.[31]

The most detailed and advanced statements can be found in the ARCIC documents. They show agreement on some form of universal primacy, and indeed its necessity for the unity of the Church, but register caution about the way that this primacy is to be exercised. "According to Christian doctrine the unity in truth of the Christian community demands visible expression. We agree that such visible expression is the will of God and that the maintenance of visible unity at the universal level includes the episcope of a universal primate. This is a doctrinal statement. But the way episcope is realized concretely in ecclesial life ... will depend upon contingent historical factors and upon development under the guidance of the Holy Spirit" (ARCIC *Authority I,* 23). This last point is given further precision in the Agreed Statement of IARC-CUM: "While some Anglicans are coming to view the ministry of the Bishop of Rome as a sign and focus of unity, there continue to be questions about whether the Petrine ministry as exercised by the Bishop of Rome exists within the Church by divine right ... " (IARCCUM *GTUM,* 75).

ARCIC II's *Gift of Authority* summarizes the progress achieved on this subject by ARCIC I as follows: "This progress can already be seen in the convergence in under-standing of authority achieved by previous ARCIC state-ments, [including] ... the need for a universal primacy exercised by the Bishop of Rome as a sign and a safeguard of unity within a re-united Church (cf. Authority in the Church II,9); the need for the universal primate to exercise his ministry in collegial association with the other bishops (cf. Authority in the Church II,9); an understanding of the universal primacy and conciliarity which complements and does not supplant the exercise of episcope in local churches (cf. Authority in the Church 1, 21-23; Authority in the Church II,19" (ARCIC *Gift,* 1). Overall, the ARCIC dialogue claims to have reached an accord on the basic principles of primacy. "This consensus is of fundamental importance. While it does not wholly resolve all the problems associated with papal primacy, it provides us with a solid basis for confronting them" (ARCIC *Authority I,* 24).

The first phase of Lutheran–Catholic dialogue did not want to overlook the question of the Petrine ministry, noting that,

"The office of the papacy as a visible sign of the unity of the church was therefore not excluded insofar as it is subordinated to the primacy of the gospel by theological reinterpretation and practical restructuring" (L–C *Malta,* 66). This dialogue continues with the observation, "The question, however, which remains controversial between Catholics and Lutherans is whether the primacy of the pope is necessary for the church, or whether it represents only a fundamentally possible function. It was nevertheless agreed that the question of altar fellowship and of mutual recognition of ministerial offices should not be unconditionally dependent on a consensus on the question of primacy" (L–C *Malta,* 66).

Continuing reflection on this matter, the second phase of dialogue states, "Also in this connection the question arises for Lutherans of service to the unity of the church at the universal level . . . While the traditional controversies have not yet been completely settled, it can nevertheless be said that Lutheran theologians today are among those who look not only to a future council or to the responsibility of theology, but also to a special Petrine office, when it is a question of service to the unity of the church at the universal level. – Much remains theologically open here, especially the question as to how this universal ministry in the service of truth and unity can be exercised, whether by a general council, or by a group, or by an individual bishop respected by all Christians. But in various dialogues, the *possibility* begins to emerge that the Petrine office of the Bishop of Rome also need not be excluded by Lutherans as a visible sign of the unity of the church as a whole, 'insofar as [this office] is subordinated to the primacy of the gospel by theological reinterpretation and practical restructuring' " (L–C *Ministry,* 73 citing L–C *Malta,* 66).

The Reformed–Catholic dialogue mentions important issues relating to this theme, but has not yet directly engaged in discussion on the specific role of the Bishop of Rome. As already seen in paragraph 64 above, the dialogue indicates agreement on the need for *episcopé* in the Church at the local, regional and universal levels (cf. *Ref II,* 142). This dialogue refers to this question, furthermore, in terms of the relationship between the Church local and universal.

In its discussion on conciliar fellowship as outlined by the WCC Assembly in Nairobi (1975), the Reformed-Catholic dialogue sees in the Nairobi declaration "a sketch of the way in which organic unity could be structured even at the universal level" (*Ref II,* 162). Having already raised the question of the office of Peter in the first phase of dialogue (cf. *Ref I,* 107), the second phase of dialogue indicated that "we have begun to come to terms with the particularly difficult issue of the structure of ministry required for communion in the universal church. . . . As we pursue the dialogue on the church's structure and ministry, this theme deserves closer attention" (*Ref II,* 143). While the Reformed–Catholic dialogue does not give significant attention to the Petrine ministry, it refers to the role of Peter in the New Testament: "It is within the normative expression of this apostolicity contained in the New Testament that a witness is given to the special ministry given by Christ to the Twelve, and to Peter within that circle of Twelve" (*Ref I,* 95). At this point, the dialogue has not gone further, and so the challenge of dealing with it still needs to be taken up.

The Catholic–Methodist dialogues reflect some of the ARCIC consensus. "Methodists accept that whatever is properly required for the unity of the whole of Christ's Church must by that very fact be God's will for his Church. A universal primacy might well serve as focus of and ministry for the unity of the whole Church" (M–C *Nairobi*, 58). The corollary of this cautious approach was then set forth: "In particular, with proper safeguards, Methodists may be prepared to receive a Petrine ministry exercised collegially within the college of bishops as a final decision-making authority in the Church, at least insofar as essential matters of faith are concerned" (M–C *Seoul*, 113). However, following careful examination of the scriptural and historical origins of the Petrine ministry (cf. M–C *Nairobi*, 41–47, 51–55), Methodists remain reticent about the universal and apostolic claims of the papacy. In their view, it "cannot be established from Scripture alone" (M–C *Nairobi*, 56) and they note that "some of the current functions carried out by the Bishop of Rome ... do not pertain to the essence of his universal ministry of unity" (M–C *Nairobi*, 59). Accordingly, the dialogue commends further joint study "on the precise nature and extent of the authority which properly belongs to the Pope's universal ministry" (M–C *Nairobi*, 62).

In conclusion it may be said that the old polemics regarding the Petrine ministry have been overcome, but full consensus is still far from sight. As regards details, the different dialogues have made different progress. There is a high degree of convergence in ARCIC and an initial openness in the Lutheran–Catholic dialogue, but more hesitancy is evident in the dialogue with the Reformed and the Methodist Churches. In all these cases it would appear that there is still a long way to go.

6. *Teaching Authority: Maintaining the Church in the Truth*

67. There is agreement among all churches and ecclesial communities that the ministry and the ministries in the

Church are not an end in themselves, but that ministry is service to preach and to teach the Gospel, and stands under the Gospel. It was one of the principal intentions of the Reformers to emphasize this point. For Luther the Church is *creatura Evangelii* (WA 2,430) and therefore subordinate to the Gospel. While recognising the *ministerium docendi evangelii* (CA V) and the power of bishops to teach and to reject doctrines contrary to the Gospel (CA XXVIII), Luther at the same time emphasized the right of the community "to judge all doctrine and to call and dismiss all teachers" (WA 11, 408-416). This point reveals the very core of our differences and the heart of ecumenical dialogues. It is an issue which forms the centre of the hermeneutical problem which has accompanied the ecumenical movement from its very beginning and is still central in it today.[32]

All dialogues agree that the whole people of God shares the responsibility of remaining faithful to the truth revealed in Jesus Christ, while a particular role and responsibility is given to those exercising *episcopé* in the Church. But reflecting on the question of teaching authority the dialogues show significant differences on the way that the common responsibility of all faithful – their consensus and reception – relates to teaching authority, on the structures of finding consensus and decision making, and on the binding character or even infallibility of such a teaching authority.

a)   Teaching authority in ARCIC

68.   ARCIC understands bishops as having a vital role in the process of discernment, bearing "a special responsibility for promoting truth and discerning error" (ARCIC *Authority I*, 18) and for preserving and promoting communion; but this is never exercised apart from the whole body of the faithful. The "interaction of bishop and people" in this exercise of

discernment and teaching "is a safeguard of Christian life and fidelity" (ARCIC *Authority I*, 18). "The task of those entrusted with oversight, acting in the name of Christ, is to foster the promptings of the Spirit and to keep the community within the bounds of the apostolic faith, to sustain and promote the Church's mission, by preaching, explaining and applying its truth. In responding to the insights of the community, and of the individual Christian, whose conscience is also molded by the same Spirit, those exercising oversight seek to discern what is the mind of Christ. Discernment involves both heeding and sifting in order to assist the people of God in understanding, articulating and applying their faith" (ARCIC *Church,* 32).

"In their concern to make the Gospel accessible to all who are open to receive it, those charged with the ministry of memory and teaching have accepted new and hitherto unfamiliar expressions of faith. ... In its continuing life, the Church seeks and receives the guidance from the Holy Spirit that keeps its teaching faithful to apostolic Tradition. Within the whole body, the college of bishops is to exercise the ministry of memory to this end. They are to discern and give teaching which may be trusted because it expresses the truth of God surely" (ARCIC *Gift,* 41–42). "The duty of maintaining the Church in the truth is one of the essential functions of the episcopal college. It has the power to exercise this ministry because it is bound in succession to the apostles, who were the body authorised and sent by Christ to preach the Gospel to all the nations. The authenticity of the teaching of individual bishops is evident when this teaching is in solidarity with that of the whole episcopal college. The exercise of this teaching authority requires that what it teaches be faithful to Holy Scripture and consistent with apostolic Tradition. This is expressed by the teaching of the Second Vatican Council,

'This teaching office is not above the Word of God, but serves it' " (ARCIC *Gift*, 44 citing the Dogmatic Constitution on Divine Revelation, *Dei verbum*, 10; cf. ARCIC *Communion*, 32).

In general, the Anglican participants in ARCIC I found the terminology of 'infallibility' unhelpful. "We agree that this is a term applicable unconditionally only to God, and that to use it of a human being, even in highly restricted circumstances, can produce many misunderstandings. That is why in stating our belief in the preservation of the Church from error we have avoided using the term" (ARCIC *Authority II*, 32). Anglicans agree with Catholics on the "indefectibility of the Church, that the Holy Spirit leads the Church into all truth" (IARCCUM *GTUM*, 76) and are willing to accept the notion of 'authoritative proclamation' (cf. ARCIC *Authority II*, 27) in terms of the Church as a whole: "Maintenance in the truth requires that at certain moments the Church can in a matter of essential doctrine make a decisive judgement which becomes part of its permanent witness" (ARCIC *Authority II*, 24).

On occasion, this function may be exercised by one person, namely, the universal primate. "The Church's judgement is normally given through a synodal decision, but at times a primate acting in communion with his fellow bishops may articulate the decision even apart from a synod. Although responsibility for preserving the Church from fundamental error belongs to the whole Church, it may be exercised on its behalf by a universal primate" (ARCIC *Authority II*, 28; cf. *Gift*, 41-43). However, Anglicans hesitate at the idea of attributing to the Bishop of Rome the authority to pronounce an infallible definition, and would insist upon the issue of reception. "In spite of our agreement over the need of a universal primacy in a united Church, Anglicans do not accept the guaranteed possession of such a gift of divine assistance in judgement necessarily attached to the office of the bishop of Rome by virtue of which his formal decisions can be known to be wholly assured before their reception by the faithful" (ARCIC *Authority II*, 31).

The dialogues show that this notion of reception is the key element in any Anglican notion of indefectibility. "Anglicans, believing that the indefectibility of the Church is preserved by fidelity to the Scriptures, the catholic creeds, the sacraments and the ministry of bishops, do not assign an infallible ministry to any group or individual within its life. They hold that doctrine, however defined, must be received by the body of believers to whom it is addressed as consonant with Scripture and Tradition" (IARCCUM *GTUM*, 76).

b)   Teaching authority in the other dialogues
69.   The Lutheran–Catholic dialogue states in its first phase, "In spite of this historical variability of proclamation, Lutherans and Catholics are convinced that the Holy Spirit unceasingly leads and keeps the church in the truth. It is in this context that one must understand the concepts of indefectibility and infallibility which are current in the Catholic tradition. These two predominantly negative concepts are subject to mis-understanding. Although they are of late origin, that to which they refer was known in the ancient church and they are based on an interpretation of New Testament texts" (L–C *Malta*, 22). "Infallibility must, first of all, be understood as a gift to the entire church as the people of God. The church's abiding in the truth should not be understood in a static way but as a dynamic event which takes place with the aid of the Holy Spirit in ceaseless battle against error and sin in the church as well as in the world" (L–C *Malta*, 23).

In the second phase the question of authority is addressed by the Lutheran–Catholic dialogue in a more differentiated way (cf. L–C *Ministry,* 50–58). Lutherans admit that the present system of decision-making by appropriate ecclesial authorities as synods – where teachers of theology together with non-ordained church members play a decisive part – creates a number of difficult problems. Accordingly, the document states, "The Lutheran churches are therefore confronted with the need to rethink the problem of the teaching office and the teaching authority. The question of the function of the episcopal ministry arises especially in this connection. On the other hand, the significance of the reception of doctrinal statements by the community and the competence of the community to judge in questions of faith must be considered" (L–C *Ministry,* 56).

The fourth phase gives a more systematic description of the ministry of teaching in Lutheran churches (cf. L–C *Apostolicity,* 376-389). It starts by saying: "Lutheran churches have no teaching office in the form of an institution in the church consisting of a particular group of individuals authorized, by belonging to the college of bishops, to issue binding judgements, and in certain circumstances ultimately binding judgements, concerning the contents of God's revelation or how doctrinal controversies are to be settled" (*Apostolicity,* 376). The document concludes: "Lutheran churches realize the teaching ministry through the collaboration of many different individuals and instances, along with an interplay of many different processes. But for Lutherans neither this complex collaboration of different instances nor a continuous line of those holding ministerial office can guarantee that the churches preserve the message of salvation in its apostolic identity. It is instead the Holy Spirit to whom the churches look for their preservation in the truth, and for this they pray.

Nonetheless, pastors exercise their teaching ministry in eschatological responsibility for the eternal salvation of those entrusted to them (Acts 10:17-26)" (*Apostolicity*, 389).

A corresponding section on the different configuration and functioning of the teaching office in Catholic doctrine (cf. *Apostolicity*, 411–428) leads to the conclusion: "Presentation by the magisterium of the truth of faith along with clarifications of the binding force of particular contents does not mean that such a presentation prevents the church in the future from finding under the lead of the Holy Spirit new formulations of its faith which correspond better to the challenges of new historical situations. The actual development of the Catholic sense of faith shows ongoing movement through crises and conflicts toward the original fullness of truth concerning God's saving work that the gospel proclaimed once and for all" (*Apostolicity*, 428).

Although stating that "the Catholic magisterium is considerably different from the functioning of teaching authority in the Lutheran churches with the office of bishops and their synodical forms" (*Apostolicity*, 449) and despite different configurations of teaching ministries (cf. *Apostolicity*, 453), in the most recent dialogues there are areas of a differentiated consensus so that the remaining differences are not to be seen as church-dividing (cf. *Apostolicity*, 431). It is possible to speak of a 'reconciled diversity' concerning (1) the existence of such a ministry or office at both local and supra-local levels, (2) the functioning of such an office, not as a monopoly, but (according to Catholic understanding) alongside various instances of witness to God's word, and (3) the combination of both constructive and critical functions in the work of teaching, whereby the teaching ministry gives an ongoing public voice to the definitive coming of God to humankind in the death and resurrection of Christ (cf. *Apostolicity,* 450–460). Here again occurs the far-reaching thesis of a 'differentiated consensus', which requires further discussion (cf. above footnote 21).[33]

70. The Reformed-Catholic dialogue focuses on Church as *creatura Verbi* and affirms, "We are agreed that as *creatura Verbi* the Church together with its Tradition stands under the living Word of God and that the preacher and teacher of the Word is to be viewed as servant of the Word (cf. Lk 1:2) and must teach only what the Holy Spirit permits him to hear in the Scriptures. This hearing and teaching takes place in a living combination with the faith, life and, above all, the worship of the community of Christ. We are agreed that the development of doctrine and the production of confessions of faith is a dynamic process. In this process the Word of God proves its own creative, critical and judging power. Through the Word, therefore, the Holy Spirit guides the Church to reflection, conversion and reform" (*Ref I,* 26).

With regard to the Catholic term 'infallibility', while "the Reformed note that the expression 'the infallibility of the Church' is almost never used in their tradition, Catholics note for their part that this word is relatively a recent one in theological terminology and seems hardly a happy term because of the maximizing interpretations to which it often gives rise. As for the theology of infallibility, apart from the fact that too often there has been a tendency to reduce the question of the infallibility of the Church to the particular problem of the infallibility of the Pope, and even to a certain manner of exercising this latter, it should be stated that it has been developed into a onesidedly juridical problem which makes it all the more irreconcilable with Reformed thinking. We are nevertheless able to formulate a certain viewpoint in common" (*Ref I,* 39). "The promise made by God to the Church is this: God remains faithful to his covenant and, despite the weaknesses and errors of Christians, he makes his Word heard in the Church" (*Ref I,* 40).

"The Reformed rejection of any infallibility which is accorded to men derives from a repugnance to bind God and the Church in this way, in view of the sovereignty of Christ over the Church and of the liberty of the Spirit, a repugnance strengthened by the experience of frequent errors and resistances to the Word on the part of the Church. In addition there is a fear lest confidence in the infallibility of a formulation should distort the personal character of faith in the living Christ; further, the fact that many Reformed take the resistance of man to the Spirit of God so seriously today that any assertion of the infallibility of the Church becomes impossible. Apart from that, for Reformed sensibility, any claim to infallibility in the modern world represents an obstacle to the credibility of the proclamation. The misgivings concerning the idea of ecclesiastical infallibility do not detract from the decisive though subordinate weight given in the Reformed tradition to the ancient Ecumenical Councils in the transmission and interpretation of the Gospel. For the Reformed, however, what alone is infallible, properly speaking, is God's fidelity to his covenant, whereby he corrects and preserves his Church by the Spirit until the consummation of his reign" (*Ref I,* 42).

According to the Reformed–Catholic dialogue, "The continuity of right doctrine is guarded by the application of Holy Scripture and transmitted by the continuity of the teaching function of the special ministry. As with all aspects of the Church's ministry, so with the particular case of apostolic succession: it requires at once a historical continuity with the original apostles and a contemporary and graciously renewed action of the Holy Spirit" (*Ref I*, 101). According to the Reformed–Catholic dialogue, "The Word of God is the primary source by which the Holy Spirit guides the discernment of the church. ... Both of our communities affirm the ultimate authority of the Word of God in discerning God's will for the church. But the paths by which we claim to have access to that Word can be quite different" (*Ref III,* 130).

71. The Methodist–Catholic dialogues point in a similar direction. "We all agree that the church's apostolicity involves continuous faithfulness in doctrine, ministry, sacrament and life to the teaching of the New Testament. In considering the ordained ministry of another church we use this faithfulness as our criterion, but we differ in the account we give of apostolic succession" (M–C *Dublin*, 84). "As the community is renewed from one Lord's Day to the next, it is nourished by the Tradition it has received, and responsibility for this is especially entrusted to those ministers who inherit the apostolic function of oversight in the community. The function of oversight entails on the part of the ministers solicitude for all the churches: they are charged to ensure that the community remain one, that it grow in holiness, that it preserve its catholicity, and that it be faithful to apostolic teaching and to the commission of evangelization given by Christ himself" (M–C *Singapore*, 74).

"There is no disagreement that the Church has authority to teach. In the Church, the revelation of God in Christ comes to us through Scripture, and to maintain God's people in the truth is the loving work of the Spirit in the Church. But this maintenance is not a matter of mere repetition of formulae. The Spirit moves the Church to constant reflection on the Scriptures which he himself inspired and on their traditional interpretation, so that she may speak with undiminished authority to men in different times and places, in different social and cultural settings, facing new and difficult problems. This is not of course to question the abiding importance of credal statements and such Conciliar pronouncements as the Chalcedonian definition. The enduring validity of these does not restrict the power of the Spirit to speak in new ways to the Church, whose living voice never speaks in isolation from its living past. It stands under the living word of God." (M–C *Honolulu*, 34).

The document *Speaking the Truth in Love. Teaching Authority among Catholics and Methodists* (*Brighton*, 2001) is a summary of the Methodist–Catholic dialogue on this issue. On the common basis of the ancient Church, Catholics continued to fulfil the ministry to maintain the truth through bishops, Councils, and the Bishop of Rome. Methodists have found the assurance of the guidance of the Spirit in godly individuals like John Wesley, in such providential events as the Reformation, and in gatherings like the early Councils and the Methodist Conferences, which formulate doctrinal statements but do not ascribe to them guaranteed freedom from error (cf. M-C *Brighton*, 19-21). "Methodists expect that Conference teaching firmly rooted in the normative sources of doctrine will be accepted. Refinement and reformation of teaching is part of an ongoing process through Conferences. When the teaching of a particular meeting of Conference is seen by the church to need better formulation, the next session of Conference is expected to carry out the task. We both agree that the Church stands in need of constant renewal in its teaching as in life" (*Brighton*, 24).

Methodists, then, also signal significant problems with the notion of infallibility, and would insist upon the prior reception of doctrinal statements. "The final judge of this agreement must be the assent of the sole People of God, and therefore Methodists, in considering the claims made for Councils and for the Pope, welcome the attention which Roman Catholic theologians are giving to the understanding of the reception of doctrine" (M–C *Nairobi,* 72; cf. *Brighton,* 39-42). Methodists and Catholics agree that there has always been a wide variety of service in the Church, carried out by lay people and ordained ministers in partnership. "The ministry of oversight (*episcope*) is of key importance among these forms of service. Pastoral oversight has always included authoritative teaching and preaching, for unity in love and unity in truth belong together. Methodists and Catholics affirm together the place within the community of believers of authoritative servants of communion and connection in love and in truth, authorised agents of discerning and proclaiming the truth of the Gospel". Whereas "[i]n the Catholic communion the college of bishops united with the Pope exercises supreme oversight, among Methodists it is Conference which exercises oversight. Within or alongside such structures of servant leadership, there have always been charismatic individuals whose personal ministry has been vital for the life of Christ's Church" (M–C *Brighton,* 51; cf. 72).

72. In conclusion it may be stated that there are many convergences in the doctrine on the ministry and teaching authority in the Church, but that the degree of convergence varies significantly in the different dialogues. On the key question of teaching the truth with authority, differences remain about its binding character, and about the participation of lay men and women in the task of discerning and determining the truth of the gospel within authoritative teaching procedures of the Church. Further dialogue is needed, but at the same time there is potential and hope for greater rapprochement and consensus.

✠ D. Reflections on Chapter Three

73. The abundance of material in the treatment of the Church in this chapter demonstrates how the issue of ecclesiology has taken the centre ground in ecumenical dialogue. It is a real achievement to affirm the possibility of overcoming many misunderstandings and shortcomings in ecclesiology, and to acknowledge that the dialogues have revisited and resolved certain polemical controversies and historical conflicts. On many questions a far-reaching common understanding of the nature and mission of the Church has been achieved, and the dialogue partners are clearly no longer where they were in the sixteenth century and the following periods of polemics and controversies.

74. **Part A** demonstrates that all four dialogues are united in agreement that the Church as people of God, Body of Christ and Temple of the Holy Spirit, is in intimate relation to the economy of the Trinity. All four dialogues confirm the unique mediation of Jesus Christ, and the role of the Holy Spirit as primary agent within the Church. This convergence has done much to lessen, or indeed dispel, the Reformation suspicion that Catholic ecclesial self-understanding obscured the sovereignty of God's action on behalf of human salvation. The dialogues have shown that the challenge of the Reformation has been an important impulse in advancing the Catholic self–understanding of the Church.

The dialogues have shown a common understanding of the mission of the Church and the intimate relationship between Christ, the Kingdom and the Church. They have shown the willingness of the participants to speak of the role of the Church as an 'effective sign of the Kingdom of God', and even as an 'instrument' and, in some cases, as a 'sacrament of salvation'. This has to be acknowledged as an important step towards a common understanding of the Church. The two models of the Church – *creatura verbi* and *sacramentum gratiae* – often in the past seen as in conflict or tension, are not only complementary but are both necessary for an adequate understanding of the Church.

In particular, the vision of the Church as communion – in keeping with the pattern of communion in the Holy Trinity – has become increasingly central in all dialogues. Focusing on the notion of the Church as *koinonia*/communion not only highlights the richness of the nature of the Church, but also helps in dealing with significant issues of historical conflict. Such a focus also gives rise to fruitful and promising approaches to overcoming old problems within a larger context, such as participation in the Word of God and in the Sacraments (especially the Eucharist) and the exercise of a universal ministry of unity. Issues such as the relationship between the individual and the community, between church ministry and lay people, men and women, are now set within a common framework, rather than seen as exclusive positions.

75. **Part B** has shown that all the dialogue partners have given fresh thought to the fundamental question of the authority of, and the relationship between, Scripture and Tradition. The dialogues emphasise the priority of Scripture while, at the same time, stressing the intimate interrelation between Scripture and Tradition. As a result, much of the historic conflict between *sola scriptura*, on the one hand, and Scripture and Tradition, on the other, has been overcome. A distinction has to be drawn between the *Tradition* (i.e., the living presence of the Gospel throughout the ages down to the present), and the many *traditions* within the Church. Tradition is understood in an integral and comprehensive way

that encompasses the doctrine, life and liturgy of the Church.[34] This provides a new basis for further discussion of the problem of Scripture and Tradition, and of the authority of the early Councils. The remaining unresolved and crucial problem is what the priority of the Scriptures means concretely, and how it can be critically brought to bear on the subject of Tradition in its comprehensive theological sense. Here the fundamental hermeneutical problem arises again.

76. **Part C** has spoken of the ministry of the Church continuing the mission and ministry of Christ. It presents ARCIC's consensus on ministry – a consensus only recently overshadowed by disagreement over women's ordination. The other dialogues reflect many of the themes of that consensus. There is a general consensus that ministry belongs to the Church of Christ and has to be seen as being within the community, while at the same time exercising its mission over against the community as sign of the priority of God's initiative and authority. There is also a consensus that ministry should be exercised in a personal, collegial and communal way. The dialogues have affirmed Catholics in the rediscovery of their own tradition of the common priesthood of all the baptised.

77. Unresolved problems arise when the question turns to the concrete form of the ministry, and the sacramental nature in the Catholic sense of ministerial ordination. Although rapprochements and common elements have emerged in responding to the pivotal question on the relation between *successio verbi* and *successio personae*, Tradition and succession, further clarification is needed on the question of episcopacy in the apostolic succession. While a convergence on the ministry of *episcopé* has been achieved, there is as yet no overall

consensus on the question of the threefold ministry, particularly on the distinction between the ministry of the bishop and that of other ministers of word and sacrament. Furthermore, the sacramental character of ordination and its distinction from the commission to other offices within the Church requires more discussion and clarification.[35] As a final point, the question of the ordination of women has now become a major issue between the Catholic Church and most of the Reformation church communities.

On the question of Petrine ministry the ARCIC dialogue shows a high degree of rapprochement and convergence. In the other dialogues it has been possible to overcome old polemics, resulting in a calmer climate for discussion. Fresh biblical approaches have been found for certain issues. In this difficult field, then, a new situation has emerged. But it must be acknowledged that despite theological rapprochement, and although personal relations with recent Popes have become more relaxed (and appreciation for their pastoral and spiritual leadership is often expressed), the path to consensus seems still to be long and difficult.

All the dialogues appreciate the importance of the need to preserve and remain steadfast in the truth of the faith. Nevertheless, the historical conflicts surrounding the notion of infallibility and the participation of lay people in the process of discerning and determining the truth of the Gospel within authoritative teaching procedures of the Church have not been satisfactorily resolved. Further dialogue is needed on this key issue of the ecumenical hermeneutical problem. On this issue Catholics could point out more clearly that the Magisterium (according to Catholic understanding) has to be seen as embedded in a process of communication with other instances and witnesses, especially liturgy, creeds,

Church Fathers, witness of the faithful, synodical structures etc.[36]

78. Notwithstanding all the important and welcome achievements, a full breakthrough in ecclesiological questions is still to come. Behind the many still unresolved individual questions can be identified one fundamental problem and one fundamental divergence in the understanding of the Church. This becomes clear when we not only ask: **What** is the Church? but also: **Where** is the Church and where is she realised in her fullness? While Protestants answer this question with the response that the Church is realized in communities in which the Word of God is correctly preached and the sacraments are duly administered (CA VII), Catholics answer that the Church of Christ subsists in (*subsistit in*) the Catholic Church, i.e., the Church is concretely, fully, permanently and effectively realised in communion with the successor of Peter and the bishops in communion with him (*LG* 8; *UR* 4).[37]

The correct interpretation of *subsistit in* has recently caused much controversy and still needs further clarification. The phrase does not signify that outside the visible confines of the Catholic Church there is no salvation or no ecclesial reality. "It is not that beyond the boundaries of the Catholic community there is an ecclesial vacuum" (*UUS* 13). Many elements of great value, which in the Catholic Church are part of the fullness of the means of salvation and of the gifts of grace which make up the Church, are also found in the other Christian communities. In these communions there exist many elements of sanctification and truth (proclamation of the Word of God, sacraments — especially baptism and the Lord's Supper — gifts of grace and charisms, etc.) (cf. *LG* 8; 15; *UR* 3 f; *UUS* 12-14). The Holy Spirit does not refrain from using these communions as means of salvation, which derive their efficacy from the very fullness of grace and truth entrusted to the Catholic Church, and since these gifts belong to the Church of Christ, they are forces impelling towards Catholic unity (cf. *UR* 3). Thus it can be summed up: "To the extent that these elements are found in other Christian communities, the one Church of Christ is effectively present in them" (*UUS* 11).

79. In the background to these affirmations there stands the fundamental ecumenical problem of the very meaning of the sacramental reality of the Church. According to Catholic understanding, the Church is a complex reality which is formed from a human and a divine element, and for this reason is compared, by no weak analogy, to the mystery of the incarnate Word. So Catholics can distinguish but cannot separate the essence of the Church from her concrete form (*Gestalt*) (cf. *LG* 8). For as Jesus Christ not only became man, but *this* man (a Jew of Nazareth of a given time, etc.), so also the Church is *this* concrete Church. As Jesus Christ in his concreteness is a *concretum universale*, so the Church has a universal meaning for all humanity, and is an eschatological foretaste and an anticipation of the universal eschatological Kingdom of God; in different degrees she is effectively present also in other ecclesial communities.

The dialogues have reflected on the sacramental character of the Church, the Church as sacrament of the Kingdom, etc. These are important breakthroughs. However, as there remain fundamental differences about the concrete structures of the Church – namely, the episcopacy in apostolic succession, primacy and the teaching authority of the episcopacy in communion with the bishop of Rome – we have not been able to come to full agreement on the precise meaning of such a sacramental structure. These remaining differences should be seen as challenges not only to our partners, but also to Catholics to deepen our own understanding of the Church and her ministries.

NOTES

16 Cf. WCC Assembly in Nairobi (1975): *What Unity Requires*; Harare (1998): *Towards a Common Understanding and Vision of the WCC*; Porto Alegre (2006): *Called to be the One Church*.

17 All these questions in a wider multilateral context are further developed in the Faith and Order Paper *The Nature and Mission of the Church. A Stage on the Way to a Common Statement*, Faith and Order Paper 198 (Geneva 2005).

18 This concept of communion emerged in the bilateral dialogues and then became prominent in the wider ecumenical context: WCC Assembly in Canberra (1991): *The Church as Koinonia: Gift and Calling*; Faith and Order in Santiago de Compostela (1993): *Message to the Churches*. Cf. Groupe des Dombes, *Pour la communion des Églises* (1988); Bilaterale Arbeitsgruppe der Deutschen Bischofskonferenz und der VELKD, *Kirchengemeinschaft in Wort und Sakrament* (1984) and ibid., *Communio Sanctorum. Die Kirche als Gemeinschaft der Heiligen* (The Church as the Communion of Saints) (2000).

19 Round X of the Lutheran–Catholic dialogue in the United States has published a wide-ranging application of the *koinonia* theme to Lutheran and Catholic ecclesiology. *The Church as Koinonia of Salvation, Its Structures and Ministries* (Washington DC 2005).

20 Still fundamental: *Baptism, Eucharist and Ministry* (part 3, chapters 4 and 6). The discussion was deepened in the German dialogue *Das kirchliche Amt in apostolischer Nachfolge I: Grundlagen und Grundfragen*. Hrsg. Von Th. Schneider-G. Wenz (Dialog der Kirchen, 12), Freiburg i. Br./Göttingen, 2004.

21 This far-reaching concept of 'differentiated consensus' or 'reconciled diversity', now applied to apostolic succession, and occurring in several parts of this text, still requires further elaboration. Its use with regard to issues which still need to be resolved calls for prior reflection on fundamental questions underlying the very concept itself. It might be better not to speak of 'differentiated consensus' but of 'convergence in significant elements', which implies that progress has been achieved and that there is hope of further rapprochement in succeeding dialogues. A more extensive treatment of this question can be found in the

German document *Das kirchliche Amt in apostolischer Nachfolge.* I-III, Hrsg. von Th. Schneider/D. Sattler und G. Wenz (Dialog der Kirchen, 12-14), Freiburg i. Br.- Göttingen 2004–2008.

22 This had already happened in the wider ecumenical context in the Faith and Order Conference in Montreal (1963) and in Louvain (1971). Montreal made the famous distinction between 'Tradition' and 'traditions' and elaborated a more comprehensive understanding of Tradition.

23 The relation between Scripture and Tradition was explicitly dealt with in the US Lutheran–Catholic dialogue: *Scripture and Tradition* (Lutherans and Catholics in Dialogue IX, Augsburg/Minneapolis 1995).

24 The most important and still fundamental document in a multilateral context on this issue is the third part of the Lima document *Baptism, Eucharist and Ministry* (1982).

25 *Ministry* and the *Elucidations* formed part of ARCIC I's *Final Report*, which was submitted for an authoritative response from the Catholic Church and the Anglican Communion. The 1988 Lambeth Conference (Resolution 8) recognized that ARCIC's work on ministry and on the Eucharist was "consonant in substance with the faith of Anglicans". The 1991 response of the Catholic Church requested further precision on several points regarding ministry and the Eucharist; this request was responded to in *Clarifications*. Cardinal Edward Cassidy, then President of the PCPCU, wrote to the Co-Chairmen of ARCIC on March 11, 1994, noting that the *Clarifications* had been "examined by the appropriate dicasteries of the Holy See" and that with regard to ministry and the Eucharist, "no further study would seem to be required at this stage".

26 For more detail on the concept of *episcopé* see next section.

27 To the degree that elements of the Church are present in the ecclesial communities, there can also be identified – as the dialogues did – elements of ministry. Therefore the question is whether *defectus ordinis* (*UR* 22) is to be understood as absence or as deficiency of the sacrament of Orders. Cf. the German document *Das kirchliche Amt in apostolischer Nachfolge.* III, Hrsg. von Th. D. Sattler und G. Wenz (Dialog der Kirchen, 12-14), Freiburg i. Br.- Göttingen 2008.

28 *Episcopé* is an ecumenical neologism introduced in order to discuss the problem of oversight independently of the controversial question of who is invested with it. Cf. Groupe des Dombes, *Le ministère episcopale* (1976); *Episkopé and Episcopate in Ecumenical Perspective*, Faith and Order Paper 102 (Geneva 1980); the LWF Statement of Lund *The Episcopal Ministry within the Apostolicity of the Church* (2003). From the Lutheran/Catholic Dialogue in Australia, see *The Ministry of Oversight. The Office of the Bishop and President in the Church* (2007).

29 Cf. the Study Document of the Joint Working Group between the Roman Catholic Church and the WCC: *The Church: Local and Universal* (1990).

30 Conciliarity (not to be confused with Conciliarism) and conciliar fellowship have become prominent issues in the wider ecumenical movement: *Conciliarity and the Future of the Ecumenical Movement* Commission on Faith and Order Louvain 1971; Salamanca Consultation, 1973; WCC Assembly, Nairobi 1975.

31 The preparatory work was undertaken by the US dialogues *Papal Primacy and the Universal Church* (Lutherans and Catholics in Dialogue V, Minneapolis 1974); *Teaching Authority and Infallibility in the Church* (Lutherans and Catholics in Dialogue VI, ibid., 1978). They were followed by the Group des Dombes: *Le ministère de communion dans l'Église universelle* (1985) and by the German document *The Condemnations of the Reformation Era: Do They Still Divide?* (1994). The Anglican Communion and many Protestant Church communities responded to the invitation of Pope John Paul II in the encyclical *Ut unum sint* (1995) (§95) to engage in a fraternal dialogue in order to find a way of exercising the primacy which, while in no way renouncing what is essential to its mission, is nonetheless open to a new situation, and to seek the forms in which this ministry may accomplish a service of love recognised by all concerned. The PCPCU gathered these contributions and made its own analysis, which it presented and discussed during the 2001 Plenary Assembly, publishing its results in *Information Service* 2002/I–II, 29–42.

32 This question was addressed on many occasions: e.g., Faith and Order Commission in Accra (1974); WCC Assembly in Nairobi (1975); Faith and Order Commission in Santiago de Compostela (1993); *A Treasure in Earthen Vessels. An Instrument for an Ecumenical Reflection on Hermeneutics*, Faith and Order Paper 182 (Geneva 1998).

33 Further deepening of these questions is found in the German document *Verbindliches Zeugnis I-III*. Hrsg. von W. Pannenberg und Th. Schneider (Dialog der Kirchen, 7, 9 and 10), Freiburg i. Br.– Göttingen 1992-98.

34 The distinction between Tradition and traditions and a more comprehensive understanding of Tradition is to be found already in the *Faith and Order* Conference in Montreal (1963).

35 The document *Ordnungsgemäß berufen* (2006) issued by the VELKD raises questions not only from the Catholic side but also within the Lutheran community itself.

36 Cf. Bilaterale Arbeitsgruppe der Deutschen Bischofskonferenz und der VELKD, *Communio Sanctorum. Die Kirche als Gemeinschaft der Heiligen* (The Church as the Communion of Saints) (2000), 11; 43 f.

37 The term *subsistit in* is contrary to the branch theory, which has been current with some Anglicans. This theory, in speaking of the Greek, Latin, Anglican and

other churches, holds that schism, even if only temporary, is internal to the Church. Some misleading understandings of the concept of sister churches tend in a similar direction. Cf. the following documents of the Congregation for the Doctrine of Faith: Note on the expression "Sister Churches" (2000); Declaration on the Unicity and Salvific Universality of Jesus Christ and the Church, *Dominus Iesus* (2000); Responses to some questions regarding certain aspects of the doctrine in the Church (2007). The controversies on the formula 'not Churches in the proper sense' and on the distinction between Church and ecclesial communities, can be lessened and seen as 'ecumenically correct', when one takes into account that the Toronto Statement of the WCC (1950) stated that the ecumenical dialogue within the WCC does not presuppose that each Church recognises the other Churches in the true and full sense as Church.

Chapter Four

The Sacraments of Baptism and Eucharist

80. According to the Reformers the Church exists as the assembly of believers *(congregatio fidelium)* among whom the word of God is purely proclaimed and the sacraments are duly administered according to the Gospel (CA VII). So for the Reformers the preaching of God's word, particularly the doctrine of justification and the response of faith, were basic for their understanding of the sacraments. Thus the sacraments were understood as included in and linked to God's word (Luther); they are testimonies, symbols, promises, seals, pledge and strengthening of faith (Calvin). According to the Reformers only the two sacraments of baptism and Eucharist (or Lord's Supper) were instituted by Jesus Christ and are therefore fundamental for the being and the life of the Church.[38] On this issue several controversies regarding the sacraments emerged at the time of the Reformation between Catholics and the Reformers, and indeed among the different Reformation movements themselves.

The sacrament of baptism was basic for all Reformers, and was not an issue of controversy with Catholics (as it was to become a question of intense debate with the Enthusiasts and the Anabaptists). For Luther, baptism is the bath of rebirth, which gives forgiveness of sins and eternal life. It encompasses the whole of Christian existence and the very being of the Church. Indeed, according to Luther, through baptism we are all made priests for sacrifice, intercession, and witness to God and his Gospel. Whoever comes out of the water of baptism can boast that he is already made a priest, bishop and pope (WA 6,407s).

The subject of the Eucharist gave rise to a passionate controversy between Catholics and the Reformers relating especially to the sacrificial character of the Eucharist. Luther called the Mass the greatest and most horrible abomination and a papal idolatry (WA 50, 200). In the same sense the reformed Catechism of Heidelberg spoke of the Mass as a denial of the once for all sacrifice and passion of Jesus Christ, defining it as an idolatry to be condemned (Question 80).[39] This strong critique had consequences for the understanding of church ministry and the meaning of the priesthood. In this context also the problem of communion under both species arose.

There were diverse positions among the Reformers concerning the real presence of Christ in the sacrament of the altar. Martin Luther retained in his teaching the real and true presence; for him the Lord's Supper is Christ's body and blood given for us. He engaged in an intense controversy with Zwingli's symbolic understanding, in the same way that Lutherans later condemned Calvin's pneumatic and actual position on a presence in the moment of holy communion. Later Melanchthon and his followers weakened Luther's realistic position, to say that Christ is not present "in, with and under bread and wine" but only "with bread and wine." However, the Catholic term 'transubstantiation' was repudiated by all Reformers.

The English Reformation remained on the margins of the continental debates but was not untouched by them. The understanding of the Eucharist ranged between a more Catholic and a more Calvinist position, a difference still evident today in High Anglican (Anglo-Catholic) and Low Church or Evangelical positions. Methodism as it arose out of the Church of England tended to retain classic Anglican positions on the true presence of Christ in the Eucharist; but its original concerns were more with spiritual renewal than doctrinal reform.

The Catholic position was defined and defended against the critique of the Reformers by the Council of Trent in its *Decree on sacraments* (with special canons on baptism and confirmation) (1547), the *Decree on the most holy Eucharist* (1551), the *Doctrine on communion under both species* (1562), and the *Doctrine on the Mass as sacrifice* (1562).

The conflicting and often polemical positions on both sides determined the nature and tone of inter-church debate in the following centuries, and are still the object of discussion – albeit in an ecumenically more relaxed spirit – today. Only with the liturgical movement in the twentieth century, the Second Vatican Council (especially the Constitution on the Liturgy *Sancrosanctum Concilium)* and the liturgical reforms in the Catholic Church and in many non–Catholic churches, has a new stage of discussion emerged.[40]

A. TOWARDS A COMMON PERSPECTIVE ON THE SACRAMENTS

81. The four dialogues do not only speak about individual sacraments but, as we have seen, also about the Church as sacrament of salvation. In this context they offer some

reflections on emerging common perspectives on the sacraments and their central role within the life of the Church.

According to the Lutheran-Catholic dialogue, "[T]he sacraments are part of God's Trinitarian act of salvation: the work that God performed in Christ once for all for the salvation of the world is mediated by the Holy Spirit, who works through word and sacrament so that *communio sanctorum* is formed, i.e., church as participation in the gifts of salvation and as communion of the faithful. ... The church lives by the word as it lives by the sacraments, and at the same time stands in their service" (L–C *Unity*, 85). "Christian life in its deepest sense is the gift of sharing in the death and resurrection of Jesus Christ. This sharing is mediated through proclamation of the word and celebration of the sacraments equally. In the sacraments it occurs in a manner which accents the corporeality, the personal character, and the community dimension of this sharing, whereby it should be noted that for Lutherans as well as for Catholics the word belongs to the nature of the sacraments themselves" (L–C *Unity*, 71; cf. *Eucharist*, 44 and 45). "Worship is rather the most important matrix of faith and an essential expression of it, for in worship our faith is induced and nourished through the proclamation of the gospel of Christ and our common sharing with others in the same gospel and the same sacramental life. In worship we are linked with Christians of every age right back to the apostles and joyfully celebrate the grace of communion with the Father and his Son Jesus Christ (cf. 1 Jn 1:3)" (L–C *Church and Justification*, 283; cf. *Eucharist*, 74 and *Apostolicity*, 272).

- The words of the Reformed–Catholic dialogue could easily be repeated by all the other dialogues: "Decades of ecumenical dialogue have produced a strong convergence on many of the essential elements of Christian liturgy" (*Ref III*, 166). The dialogues agree that the liturgy is central for the life of the Church. "The liturgy provides a privileged place where the Word is contemplated and celebrated in worship and sacrament. Thus the 'rule of worship' (*lex orandi*) is also a most important 'rule of faith' (*lex credendi*)" (*Ref III*, 137; cf. 121; 169, 175; cf. *Ref I*, 89). "Sharing word and sacrament in the presence of the Triune God, the church discovers anew its own nature as a communion and becomes what it is: the people of God, the body of Christ and the temple of the Holy Spirit (cf. Eph 2:21)" (*Ref III*, 165). There is convergence among the dialogues in describing sacraments as "visible sign[s] through which the grace of God is given by the Holy Spirit in the Church" (ARCIC *Ministry Elucidation*, 3) or as "vehicles of the unique grace of Christ mediated ultimately by Christ alone" (*Ref III*, 194; cf. M–C *Nairobi*, 13). "The transformation of the world occurs in part through efforts to create a more just and peaceful society. But Christians also believe that this transformation is realized now, in an anticipatory way, in that communion between God and human beings which takes place in the church, especially through the proclamation of the Word, the celebration of the sacraments of baptism and eucharist and other sacraments or rites" (*Ref III*, 191; cf. 30 and 47).

According to the Anglican-Catholic dialogue, "[t]he Church is intended to be the 'sacrament' of God's saving work ... Its mission is rooted in the saving mission of the Son and the Spirit and is, indeed, a sacramental form of that divine mission" (IARCCUM *GTUM*, 16). "Both the Roman Catholic Church and the Churches of the Anglican Communion are liturgical Churches in which God is glorified in common public worship" (IARCCUM *GTUM*, 100).

The Methodist-Catholic dialogue looks towards the very heart of the sacraments. "The Mystery of the Word made flesh and the sacramental mystery of the eucharist point towards a view of the Church based upon the sacramental idea, i.e., the Church takes its shape from the Incarnation from which it originated and the eucharistic action by which its life is constantly being renewed" (M–C *Nairobi,* 10). "Baptism initiates the individual into the *koinonia* of the Church; in the eucharist Christ is really present to the believer (cf. M-C *Dublin* 54), who is thus bound together in *koinonia* both with the Lord and with others who share the sacramental meal" (M–C *Nairobi,* 12). "It is by divine institution that the Church has received baptism and the eucharist, outward signs of inward grace consisting of actions and words by which God encounters his people" (M–C *Nairobi,* 13). "In the celebration of the eucharist, as both word and table, the Church is built up as the body of Christ" (M–C *Rio,* 100; cf. 118).

B. COMMON UNDERSTANDING OF BAPTISM

82. Baptism is central and fundamental in the New Testament. Because it was not at the centre of Reformation controversies, it has not been a central focus of the dialogues as such. Nonetheless, because of the separation of the ecclesial communities, each other's baptisms were not always recognized in practice, as indicated by cases of rebaptism.

Today the partners in the dialogues are able to agree clearly about baptism and express a common understanding about the institution of baptism by Jesus Christ, baptism with water and in the trinitarian formula, baptism as incorporation in Christ and gift of the new life in Christ. They regard baptism as a source of unity binding separated Christians to one another, and they express mutual recognition of baptism. This is fundamental for the ecumenical dialogue and for acknowledging each other as brothers and sisters in Christ.[41]

The second chapter of this document has outlined the consensus on justification. That consensus includes, in numbers 25 and 28 of the *JDDJ*, two significant areas of agreement on Baptism: by the action of the Holy Spirit in baptism, the sinner is granted the gift of salvation (cf. 25). "We confess together that in baptism the Holy Spirit unites one with Christ, justifies, and truly renews the person" (28). This consensus is also shared by all the other dialogue partners, as illustrated in the following examples.

"Lutherans and Catholics are conscious that they participate in one and the same baptism. In keeping with the statement *BEM*, we jointly confess that 'Christian baptism is rooted in the ministry of Jesus of Nazareth, in his death and in his resurrection. It is incorporation into Christ, who is the crucified and risen Lord; it is entry into the new covenant between God and God's people'" (L–C *Unity*, 75 citing *BEM, Baptism,* I.1; cf. 71). "Baptised by the one Spirit into the one body (cf. 1 Cor 12:13) believers – nourished by the body of Christ – become ever more one body through the Holy Spirit (cf. 1 Cor 10:17)" (L–C *Eucharist,* 25; cf. *Ministry,* 13; *Church and Justification,* 35 and 68). "Baptism in the name of the Father, Son and Holy Spirit leads us into communion with the triune God and into sharing in his blessings and thus also knits believers together into a communion" (L–C *Church and Justification,* 68). "The growing reciprocal recognition as church [because of baptism and other ecclesial factors] thus leads us to binding common life, to active exchange, and to mutual acceptance in witness, service and solidarity according to the nature of the church as 'people of God', 'body of Christ', and 'temple of the Holy Spirit'. It commits our churches at both the local and the universal levels not only to an occasional fellowship, practised from time to time, but to a fully lived-out fellowship that requires for its realization a structured form" (L–C *Unity*, 91).

The Reformed-Catholic dialogue reached similar formulations. "We have discovered anew that the Roman Catholic Church and the Reformed Churches are bound by manifold ties. Both communions confess Jesus Christ as Lord and Saviour, affirm the Trinitarian faith of the apostolic Church through the ages, and observe the one Baptism into the threefold Name" (*Ref II,* 4; cf. *Ref I,* 79 and 96). "Recognizing [because of baptism and other ecclesial factors] that despite continuing divisions a real though imperfect communion already exists between Reformed and Roman Catholic Christians, what implications does this communion have for our understanding of the continuity of the church?" (*Ref II,* 124). "Our churches should give expression to mutual recognition of Baptism. In some countries, the Roman Catholic and Reformed Churches have already agreed to accept each other's Baptism fully and without reserve, provided that it has been celebrated in the name of the Father, the Son and the Holy Spirit and with the use of water. We believe that such agreements can and should be made in all places without delay. Such an agreement implies that under no circumstances can there be a repetition of baptism which took place in the other church. Mutual recognition of baptism is to be understood as an expression of the profound communion that Jesus Christ himself establishes among his disciples and which no human failure can ever destroy" (*Ref II,* 152).

"Anglicans and Roman Catholics agree that they receive one baptism, administered with water in the name of the Father, the Son, and the Holy Spirit. We do this in obedience to the command of the risen Lord (cf. Matthew 28.18–20)" (IARCCUM *GTUM,* 33). "We consider baptism a sacrament of initiation instituted by Jesus Christ, by which we are incorporated into the life of his body, the Church. Baptism is the sacrament of faith, through which a person embraces the faith of the Church and is embraced by it" (*GTUM* 33). "We believe that all who are baptised are incorporated into the body of Christ, the Church. 'Through baptism, Christians are brought into union with Christ, with each other and with the Church of every time and place' " (*GTUM* 36 citing *BEM, Baptism,* 6). "The Anglican Communion and the Catholic Church recognise the baptism each confers. Anglicans and Catholics therefore regard our common baptism as the basic bond of unity between us, even as we recognise that the fullness of eucharistic communion to which baptism should lead is impeded by disagreement concerning some of the elements of faith and practice which we acknowledge are necessary for full, visible communion" (*GTUM* 38). "Anglicans and Catholics are committed to overcoming by God's grace all the divisions that still hinder the fullness of eucharistic and ecclesial communion. Our fundamental baptismal communion gives us the shared responsibility to witness as fully as possible to the Gospel of Christ before the world and to show forth the new life lived by the body of Christ, with the liberation and renewal it brings" (*GTUM* 38).

"Through the ministry of the Church baptism is given with water 'in the name of the Father, the Son, and the Holy Spirit.' Baptism is irrevocable and is not repeated. While it is received in the context of a local church and in a specific Christian community, it introduces people into the universal

Church of Christ and the gathering of the saints" (M–C *Rio*, 101; cf. 8; *Singapore*, 63; *Seoul*, 155). "Those who are baptised receive a share in the death of the one Lord Jesus Christ and in the power of his resurrection; at the same time they are baptised into the one body, the body of Christ with its many members who suffer and rejoice together" (M–C *Rio*, 118; cf. *Seoul*, 144). "By baptism, and the faith in Christ which it signifies, Catholics and Methodists already enjoy a certain measure of ecclesial communion. The purpose of the dialogue between us is to increase and deepen our relationship until we reach sufficient agreement in the Christian truth that our common baptism can without equivocation be completed in our mutual participation in the Meal to which the one Lord invites us and all his followers" (M–C *Rio*, 10). "We encourage ongoing discussion at the appointed levels wherever formal mutual recognition of baptism between our churches is still lacking. We are happy that this recognition has already taken place in many regions" (M–C *Rio*, 119). Methodist-Catholic dialogue makes reference to the regeneration brought about by Baptism. "Baptism is given in the midst of the community to new Christians who, at their baptism, confess the faith they have received. ... United to Christ in his dying and in his rising, they bear witness that they are reborn in him" (M–C *Singapore*, 63).

C. THE EUCHARIST

1. Consensus on Eucharist in the Anglican–Catholic Dialogue

83. All the dialogues have given their attention to questions relating to the Eucharist. However, the consensus in the statements of the ARCIC dialogue has received official

acknowledgment; through a lengthy process of agreed statements by ARCIC, official responses and further clarifications, a "substantial agreement" on essential points of eucharistic doctrine has been achieved.[42] While "no attempt was made to present a fully comprehensive treatment of the subject", the Commission's conviction was that "nothing essential has been omitted" (ARCIC *Eucharist*, Preface). ARCIC noted its belief that the consensus reached on the nature of the Eucharist was "consonant with biblical teaching and with the tradition of our common inheritance" (*Eucharist*, 1)

a)   *The centrality of the Eucharist in the life of the Church*

84.   Anglicans and Catholics understand the Eucharist as central to the life of the Church, nurturing and deepening the new relationship between God and humanity made possible by the saving life, death and resurrection of Jesus Christ (cf. ARCIC *Eucharist*, 2). "Christ through the Holy Spirit in the eucharist builds up the life of the Church, strengthens its fellowship and furthers its mission. The identity of the Church as the body of Christ is both expressed and effectively proclaimed by its being centred in, and partaking of, his body and blood. In the whole action of the eucharist, and in and by his sacramental presence given through bread and wine, the crucified and risen Lord, according to his promise, offers himself to his people" (ARCIC *Eucharist*, 3). Along with baptism, the Eucharist is understood as a sacrament "necessary to salvation" (ARCIC *Ministry Elucidation*, 3).

The Eucharist is central to the *mission* of the Church. "When we gather around the same table in this communal meal at the invitation of the same Lord and when we 'partake of the one loaf', we are one in commitment not only to Christ and to one another, but also to the mission of the Church in the world" (ARCIC *Eucharist*, 4). It is both a sign and a means of building up the *unity of the body of Christ*; it is "the effectual sign of *koinonia*" and "the sacrament of Christ, by which he builds up and nurtures his people in the *koinonia* of his body. By the eucharist all the baptized are brought into communion with the source of *koinonia*" (ARCIC *FR Introduction*, 6; cf. *Eucharist*, 6). The Eucharist also has an eschatological dimension, and is a *foretaste of the Kingdom*. "In the eucharist we proclaim the Lord's death until he comes. Receiving a foretaste of the kingdom to come, we look back with thanksgiving to what Christ has done for us, we greet him present among us, we look forward to his final appearing in the fullness of his kingdom ..." (ARCIC *Eucharist*, 4; cf. 11).

b)   *Eucharist: memorial and sacrifice*

85.   In formulating a common understanding of the sacrificial character of the Eucharist, ARCIC reflects in detail upon the notion of the Eucharist as *memorial*. "Christ's redeeming death and resurrection took place once and for all in history. Christ's death on the cross, the culmination of his whole life of obedience, was the one, perfect and sufficient sacrifice for the sins of the world. There can be no repetition of or addition to what was then accomplished once for all by Christ. Any attempt to express a nexus between the sacrifice of Christ and the eucharist must not obscure this fundamental fact of the Christian faith. Yet God has given the eucharist to his Church as a means through which the atoning work of Christ on the cross is proclaimed and made effective in the life of the Church. The notion of *memorial* as understood in the passover celebration at the time of Christ − i.e. the making effective in the present of an event in the past − has opened the way to a clearer understanding of the relationship between Christ's sacrifice and the eucharist. The eucharistic memorial is no mere calling to mind of a past event or of its significance, but the Church's effectual proclamation of God's mighty acts.

Christ instituted the eucharist as a memorial (*anamnesis*) of the totality of God's reconciling action in him. In the eucharistic prayer the Church continues to make a perpetual memorial of Christ's death, and his members, united with God and one another, give thanks for all his mercies, entreat the benefits of his passion on behalf of the whole Church, participate in these benefits and enter into the movement of his self-offering" (ARCIC *Eucharist*, 5; cf. 3).[43] In the *Clarifications* offered by ARCIC in 1993, the Commission affirmed its "belief that the eucharist is truly a sacrifice, but in a sacramental way", and that the propitiatory nature of the eucharistic sacrifice also applies to the faithful departed.

c)   *Real presence of Christ in the Eucharist*

86.   Anglicans and Catholics are in agreement that "Communion with Christ in the eucharist presupposes his true presence, effectually signified by the bread and wine which, in this mystery, become his body and blood" (ARCIC *Eucharist*, 6).[44] "The elements are not mere signs; Christ's body and blood become really present and are really given" (*Eucharist*, 9). "What is here affirmed is a sacramental presence in which God uses realities of this world to convey the realities of the new creation: bread for this life becomes the bread of eternal life. Before the eucharistic prayer, to the question: 'What is that?', the believer answers: 'It is bread'. After the eucharistic prayer, to the same question he answers: 'It is truly the body of Christ, the Bread of Life' " (*Eucharist Elucidation*, 6).

In a footnote, ARCIC notes: "The word *transubstantiation* is commonly used in the Roman Catholic Church to indicate that God acting in the eucharist effects a change in the inner reality of the elements. The term should be seen as affirming the *fact* of Christ's presence and of the mysterious and radical change which takes place. In contemporary Roman Catholic theology it is not understood as explaining *how* the change takes place" (ARCIC *Eucharist,* 6). *Clarifications* returns to this point when asked if the text was expressing "certitude that Christ is present sacramentally and substantially" in the consecrated elements. Noting that Paul VI, in *Mysterium Fidei*, acknowledged "the legitimacy of fresh ways of expressing this change even by using new words, provided that they kept and reflected what transubstantiation was intended to express", the *Clarifications* proceeded to state: "This has been our method of approach. In several places the Final Report indicates its belief in the presence of the living Christ truly and really in the elements. Even if the word 'transubstantiation' only occurs in a footnote, the Final Report wished to express what the Council of Trent, as evident from its discussions, clearly intended by the use of the term" (ARCIC *Clarifications*).

ARCIC is careful to situate the real presence of Christ in the Eucharist within the context of the paschal mystery and God's desire to transform all of humanity through it: "The real presence of his body and blood can, however, only be understood within the context of the redemptive activity whereby he gives himself, and in himself reconciliation, peace and life, to his own. On the one hand, the eucharistic gift springs out of the paschal mystery of Christ's death and resurrection, in which God's saving purpose has already been definitively realized. On the other hand, its purpose is to transmit the life of the crucified and risen Christ to his body, the Church, so that its members may be more fully united with Christ and with one another" (ARCIC *Eucharist,* 6; cf. 9).

According to ARCIC, faith is required for the reception of the Eucharist to result in a lifegiving and transforming encounter with the Lord. "The sacramental body and blood of the Saviour are present as an offering to the believer awaiting his welcome.

When this offering is met by faith, a lifegiving encounter results. Through faith Christ's presence – which does not depend on the individual's faith in order to be the Lord's real gift of himself to his Church – becomes no longer just a presence *for* the believer, but also a presence *with* him" (ARCIC *Eucharist,* 8; cf. *Eucharist Elucidation*, 7; IARCCUM *GTUM*, 42).

d) Epiclesis *rediscovered*

87. The epiclesis, that is, the invocation of the Holy Spirit upon the gifts of bread and wine, was for a long time a point of controversy between the Eastern and the Western churches. The ecumenical movement has helped to overcome this disagreement and has contributed to the acceptance by most western traditions of the role of the Spirit in the transformation of the eucharistic species into the body and blood of the Lord. This development is also echoed in all four dialogues, and is a notable achievement for all dialogue partners.

ARCIC makes brief but clear mention of the work of the Holy Spirit in the Eucharist. "According to the traditional order of the liturgy the consecratory prayer (*anaphora*) leads to the communion of the faithful. Through this prayer of thanksgiving, a word of faith addressed to the Father, the bread and wine become the body and blood of Christ by the action of the Holy Spirit, so that in communion we eat the flesh of Christ and drink his blood" (ARCIC *Eucharist*, 9). "The Lord who thus comes to his people in the power of the Holy Spirit is the Lord of glory. In the eucharistic celebration we anticipate the joys of the age to come. By the transforming action of the Spirit of God, earthly bread and wine become heavenly manna and the new wine, the eschatological banquet for the new man: elements of the first creation become pledges and first fruits of the new heaven and the new earth" (*Eucharist,* 11; cf. *Clarifications*; *Church*, 17).

e) *The ordained minister of the Eucharist*

88. Anglicans and Catholics say together: "To proclaim reconciliation in Christ and to manifest his reconciling love belong to the continuing mission of the Church. The central act of worship, the eucharist, is the memorial of that reconciliation and nourishes the Church's life for the fulfilment of its mission. Hence it is right that he who has oversight in the Church and is the focus of its unity should preside the celebration of the eucharist. Evidence as early as Ignatius show that at least in some churches, the man exercising this oversight presided at the eucharist and no other could do so without his consent (*Letter to the Smyrnaeans*, 8,1)" (ARCIC *Ministry*, 12). "Because the eucharist is the memorial of the sacrifice of Christ, the action of the presiding minister in reciting again the words of Christ at the Last Supper and distributing to the assembly the holy gifts is seen to stand in a sacramental relation to what Christ himself did offering his own sacrifice. So our two traditions commonly used priestly terms in speaking about the ordained ministry. Such language does not imply any negation of the once-for-all sacrifice of Christ by any addition or repetition" (*Ministry,* 13).

"Ordination denotes entry in this apostolic and God-given ministry, which serves and signifies the unity of the local churches in themselves and with one another. Every individual act of ordination is therefore an expression and extension of the continuing apostolicity and catholicity of the whole Church. Just as the original apostles did not choose themselves but were chosen and commissioned by Jesus, so those who are ordained are called by Christ in the Church and through the Church. Not only is their vocation from Christ but their qualification for exercising such a ministry is the gift of the Spirit.....This is expressed in ordination, when the bishop prays God to grant the gift of the Holy Spirit and lays hands on the candidate as outward sign of the gifts bestowed" (*Ministry,* 14). In this sacramental act the gift of God is bestowed upon the ministers, with the promise of divine grace for their work and their sanctification." (*Ministry,* 15).

Later on the dialogue made all this more precise: "It is only the ordained minister who presides at the eucharist, in which, in the name of Christ and on behalf of his Church, he recites the narrative of the institution of the Last Supper, and invokes the Holy Spirit upon the gifts" (*Ministry Elucidation,* 2). Also the expression "sacramental act" was given more clarity as "visible sign through which the grace of God is given by the Holy Spirit in the Church." "Both traditions affirm the pre-eminence of baptism and the eucharist as sacraments 'necessary for salvation'. This does not diminish their understanding of the sacramental nature of ordination, as to which there is no significant disagreement between them" (*Ministry Elucidation,* 3).

f) *Issues for further study*
89. In offering its synthesis of the consensus between Anglicans and Catholics on eucharistic doctrine, IARCCUM's *GTUM* also noted two issues where further dialogue was needed. Firstly, "Anglicans and Catholics acknowledge that there is an intrinsic relationship between sharing the Eucharist and full ecclesial communion, but diverge on the way in which that is expressed on the way to full communion. Churches of the Anglican Communion and the Roman Catholic Church therefore have different disciplines for eucharistic sharing" (IARCCUM *GTUM,* 46; cf. 47–48). Secondly, while "[a]doration of Christ in the reserved sacrament is encouraged in the Roman Catholic Church" and "is also practised in some Anglican churches, there are some Anglicans who would find difficulty in these devotional practices because it is feared that they obscure the true goal of the sacrament"

(IARCCUM *GTUM,* 49; cf. ARCIC *Eucharist Elucidation* 8–9; ARCIC *Clarifications*).

The Anglican-Catholic dialogue has only briefly addressed the sacramental character of confirmation, anointing of the sick, penance/reconciliation, and marriage, in the context of IARCCUM's overview of areas of agreement and continuing differences. While a degree of agreement is registered in *GTUM* 39, 81-82 and 85, the text also acknowledges divergences with regard to both reconciliation and marriage. "Anglicans and Catholics have a different practice in respect of private confession. 'The Reformers' emphasis on the direct access of the sinner to the forgiving and sustaining Word of God led Anglicans to reject the view that private confession before a priest was obligatory, although they continued to maintain that it was a wholesome means of grace, and made provision for it in the Book of Common Prayer for those 'with an unquiet and sorely troubled conscience' (citing *Life in Christ,* 46). Anglicans express this discipline in the short formula 'all may, none must, some should' " (IARCCUM *GTUM,* 86 a).

2. Eucharist in the other Dialogues

90. The other three dialogues, addressing the Eucharist, touch on several of the same themes which comprise the ARCIC consensus. They also speak of the centrality of the Eucharist in the Church, the themes of *anamnesis/memorial* and *epiclesis,* and the real presence of Christ. However, individual dialogues sometimes speak of the interrelation of these themes in different ways, and therefore study of each dialogue is necessary in order to appreciate its approach.

a)   *The centrality of the Eucharist in the life of the Church*

91. From its beginning the Lutheran–Catholic dialogue empha-
     sized the central importance of the Eucharist for the *unity* of
     the Church (cf. L–C *Eucharist,* 1), for its *mission* (cf. *Eucharist,*
     39) and for its being a sign of *eternal glory* (cf. *Eucharist,* 43).
     "The Lord's Supper is a Mystery of faith in the fullest sense of
     the word. It belongs to the all-encompassing and incompre-
     hensible mystery of salvation and participates in its character
     as mystery" (*Eucharist,* 7). "Finally, the mystery of the
     Eucharist unites us to the ultimate mystery from, through
     and towards which all things exist: the mystery of the triune
     God" (*Eucharist,* 11). "The Eucharist is thus at once the
     source and climax of the church's life. Without the
     eucharistic community there is no full ecclesial community,
     and without the ecclesial community, there is no real
     eucharistic community" (*Eucharist,* 26; cf. 25, 27, 28).

The Reformed–Catholic dialogue reflected, "The Eucharist
is a source and criterion for the renewal of the Church. The
Church's renewed understanding of the Eucharist may lead to
a renewed way of celebrating the Eucharist, revealing the
Church more clearly as essentially 'the Eucharistic community'. ... The renewal of the Church through the Eucharist
includes a continuous summons to church unity. ... At the
same time the Eucharist requires and inspires the Church's
sense of her vocation to bring the Gospel to the whole world
in proclaiming the good news of God's salvation and
exercising the work of reconciliation in its deeds. ...
Renewal, unity and mission are inseparable characteristics
of the Church as it receives in faith the gift of the Eucharist"
(*Ref I,* 88; cf. 75 and 86). "Through partaking in the
eucharist 'the Church is built up as the Body of Christ' "
(*Ref I,* 82; cf. *Ref I,* 73).

The Methodist–Catholic dialogue has expressed the centrality of the Eucharist in the life of the Church in numerous ways. "Methodists and Catholics are already agreed … that when the Eucharist is celebrated, we hear afresh the Word of God spoken to us; we enter together more deeply into the saving mystery of Christ; we encounter Christ anew in a way which ensures the living presence of Christ at the heart of the Church; we are anointed by the transforming love which is God's Holy Spirit and become more truly the Body of Christ; we are sent forth together in Christ to share more deeply in God's work in our world; and we share together a foretaste of the heavenly banquet. As we celebrate the Eucharist, called together by the Father, the Risen Lord makes us more fully what he wills his Church to be, by the power of the Holy Spirit" (M–C Seoul, 94; cf. 93; cf. M–C Dublin, 52). Methodists and Catholics are agreed in speaking of the centrality of the Eucharist, also in a way that signifies and strengthens the *unity* and *mission* of the Church (cf. M–C Denver, 83; Dublin, 73; Nairobi, 12; Rio, 100, 118), and that recognises its *eschatological* dimension (cf. M–C Rio, 102; cf. Seoul, 103; Dublin, 52).

b)   Eucharist: memorial and sacrifice

92. Concerning the once highly controversial topic of the sacrificial character of the Eucharist the Lutheran–Catholic dialogue made its own a passage from Faith and Order's Accra statement of 1974: "Christ instituted the Eucharist, sacrament of his body and blood with its focus upon the cross and resurrection, as the *anamnesis* of the whole of God's reconciling action in him. Christ himself with all that He has accomplished for us and for all creation (in his incarnation, servanthood, ministry, teaching, suffering, sacrifice, resurrection, ascension and Pentecost) is present in this *anamnesis* as is also the foretaste of his *Parousia* and the fulfilment of the Kingdom" (L–C Eucharist, 17). With regard

to the ARCIC definition the document declares: "The notion of memorial as understood in the Passover celebration at the time of Christ – i.e. the making effective in the present of an event in the past – has opened the way to a clearer understanding of the relationship between Christ's sacrifice and the Eucharist" (L–C *Eucharist*, 36).

"Catholic and Lutheran Christians together recognize that in the Lord's Supper Jesus Christ 'is present as the Crucified who died for our sins and rose again for our justification, as the once–for–all sacrifice for the sins of the world.' This sacrifice can be neither continued, nor repeated, nor replaced, nor complemented; but rather it can and should become effective ever anew in the midst of the congregation. There are different interpretations among us regarding the nature and extent of this effectiveness" (L–C *Eucharist*, 56).[45]

According to the Reformed–Catholic dialogue, "As often as we come together in the Church to obey our Lord's command to 'do this in anamnesis of me', he is in our midst. This is the presence of the Son of God who for us men and for our salvation became man and was made flesh" (*Ref I*, 82). "When Christ gives the apostles the commission 'Do this in remembrance of me!' the word 'remembrance' means more than merely a mental act of 'recalling' " (*Ref I*, 70; cf. 81). "In its joyful prayer of thanksgiving, 'in the Eucharist', when the Church of Christ remembers his reconciling death for our sins and for the sins of the whole world, Christ himself is present, who 'gave himself up on our behalf as an offering and sacrifice whose fragrance is pleasing to God' (Eph 5:2). Sanctified by his Spirit, the Church, through, with and in God's son, Jesus Christ, offers itself to the Father. It thereby becomes a living sacrifice of thanksgiving, through which God is publicly praised (cf. Rom 12:1; 1 Petr 2:5). The validity, strength and effect of the Supper are rooted in the cross of the Lord and in his living presence in the Holy Spirit. Far from bypassing us, they are fulfilled in our faith, love and service" (*Ref I,* 81; cf. 87; cf. also 69 and 75).

The Methodist–Catholic dialogue noted that there are "differences in language and emphasis", but that "we have a clear measure of agreement" (M–C *Dublin,* 62). "We are one in affirming that 'the Eucharist is the celebration of Christ's full, perfect and sufficient sacrifice, offered once and for all, for the whole world' (citing British Methodist–Catholic Proceedings, § 83, pp.56–57). It is a memorial (*anamnesis*). It is not 'a mere calling to mind of a past event or of its significance, but the Church's effectual proclamation of God's mighty acts' " (M–C *Dublin,* 63 citing at end ARCIC *Eucharist,* 5; cf. M–C *Denver,* 83). "With the whole Christian tradition Methodists and Catholics ... agree that Jesus Christ instituted the eucharist as a holy meal, the memorial of his sacrifice. As the baptized partake of it they share the sacrament of his body given for them and his blood shed for them; they present and plead his sacrifice before God the Father; and they receive the fruits of it in faith" (M–C *Rio,* 102). "In this celebration we share in Christ's offering Himself in obedience to the Father's will" (M–C *Denver,* 83).

c)   *Real presence of Christ in the Eucharist*
93.   The Lutheran–Catholic dialogues notes, "In the sacrament of the Lord's Supper Jesus Christ, true God and true man, is present wholly and entirely, in his body and blood, under the signs of bread and wine. Through the centuries Christians have attempted various formulations to describe this presence. Our confessional documents have in common affirmed that Jesus Christ is 'really', 'truly' and 'substantially' present in this sacrament... Our traditions have spoken of this presence as

'sacramental'', 'supernatural' and 'spiritual'. These terms have different connotations in the two traditions, but they have in common a rejection of a spatial or natural manner of presence, and a rejection of an understanding of the sacrament as only commemorative or figurative" (L–C *Eucharist*, 16). Nevertheless, as we shall see, there are remaining issues.

With regard to the Reformed–Catholic dialogue we read, "Thus we gratefully acknowledge that both traditions, Reformed and Roman Catholic, hold to the belief in the Real Presence of Christ in the Eucharist; and both hold at least that the Eucharist is, among other things: (1) a memorial of the death and resurrection of the Lord; (2) a source of loving communion with him in the power of the Spirit (hence the epiclesis in the Liturgy), and (3) a source of the eschatological hope for his coming again" (*Ref I*, 91; cf. *Ref II*, 152; *Ref I*, 70; *Ref I*, 82). "[T]he specific presence of Jesus Christ in the Eucharist . . . is at once sacramental and personal. He comes to us clothed in his Gospel and saving passion, so that our partaking of him is communion in his body and blood (John 6:47–56; 1 Cor 10:17). This presence is sacramental in that it is the concrete form which the mystery of Christ takes in the eucharistic communion of his body and blood. It is also personal presence because Jesus Christ in his own person is immediately present, giving himself in his reality both as true God and true Man. In the Eucharist he communicates himself to us in the whole reality of his divinity and humanity – body, mind and will, and at the same time he remains the Son who is in the Father as the Father is in him" (*Ref I*, 83; cf. 84; cf. also 76 and 79).

The Methodist–Catholic dialogue states, "Christ, in the fullness of his being, human and divine, is present in the eucharist; this presence does not depend on the experience of the communicant, but it is only by faith that we become aware of it. This is a distinctive mode of the presence of Christ; it is mediated through the sacred elements of bread and wine, which within the eucharist are efficacious signs of the body and blood of Christ" (M–C *Dublin,* 54; cf. *Denver,* 83). The Methodist–Catholic dialogue cites ARCIC in recording its agreement that "Communion with Christ in the eucharist presupposes his true presence, effectually signified by the bread and wine…" (M–C *Dublin,* 55 citing ARCIC *Eucharist,* 6).

d)   Epiclesis *rediscovered*

94.   As in the Anglican–Catholic dialogue, so in the other dialogues there is a new awareness of the relevance of the work of the Holy Spirit in the Eucharist. The Lutheran–Catholic dialogue comments that as Jesus Christ in his life on earth did all things in the Holy Spirit and as in the power of the Spirit he offered himself as sacrifice, it is also through the Holy Spirit that Christ is at work in the Eucharist. In the liturgy this becomes particularly clear in the invocation of the Holy Spirit (cf. L-C *Ministry,* 21). "In remembrance of the intercession of Christ, its high priest, the church asks with confidence, in order to be renewed and sanctified through the eucharistic gifts and strengthened to accomplish its mission in the world. In the power of the Holy Spirit the bread and wine become the body and blood of Christ through the creative word. The spirit of love causes the sacrament of love to become real in that the divine love seeks us in our earthly reality in order to bring us home again" (*Ministry,* 22). "The Eucharist is not an automatic means for the salvation of the world; it presupposes the presence of the Holy Spirit within the believers" (*Ministry,* 23).

The Reformed-Catholic dialogue also mentions the work of the Spirit in the Eucharist. "The validity, strength and effect of the Supper are rooted in the cross of the Lord and in his living presence in the Holy Spirit" (*Ref I*, 81). "The realization of this presence of Christ to us and of our union and incorporation with him is the proper work of the Holy Spirit, which takes place in the eucharistic celebration as the church calls upon the Father to send down his Spirit to sanctify both the worshipping people and the bread and wine. How Christ is present in the Eucharist, we may apprehend to a certain extent by looking at the work of the same Holy Spirit, e.g. in the birth of Jesus of the Virgin Mary and in his resurrection in body from the grave – although as acts of God they are explicable only from the side of God and not from the side of man" (*Ref I*, 82). " [I]n his self-offering to the Father through the eternal Spirit (*cf. Heb. 9,14*), he offers us also in himself and so through our union with him we share in that self-offering made on our behalf. It is the same Spirit who cries 'Abba, Father' (*cf. Mk 14,36*) in him who cries in us, as we in the Eucharist take the Lord's Prayer in our own mouth (*Rom 8,15 f., 26*)" (*Ref I*, 85).

In the Methodist–Catholic dialogue the work of the Spirit and the life in the Spirit is of great importance (cf. particularly *Honolulu*). For both dialogue partners "[t]he sacraments are effective signs by which God gives grace through faith. Their efficacy should not be conceived in any merely mechanical way. God works through his Spirit in a mysterious way beyond human comprehension, but he invites a full and free response" (M–C *Nairobi*, 15). "Those actions of the church that we call sacraments are effective signs of grace because they are not merely human acts. By the power of the Holy Spirit, they bring into our lives the life-giving action and even the self-giving of Christ himself" (*Nairobi, 16*; cf. *Rio, 51*).

e) *The ordained minister of the Eucharist*

95. All the dialogues speak of the ordained minister as the proper minister of the eucharist.[46]

> "Only through Christ Jesus does the Eucharist exist. From him comes the commission to celebrate it ever anew. Through him those who preside over the eucharistic celebration in his name are called and commissioned. The congregation is not proprietor of the action it is performing; it is not the master of the eucharist but receives it from Another, Christ living in his Church" (L–C *Eucharist*, 13). "Catholics and Lutheran Christians are of the conviction that the celebration of the Eucharist involves the leadership of a minister appointed by the church" (*Eucharist*, 65). "According to Lutheran doctrine as well, the eucharistic service is led by ordained ministers. It is 'the task of the ministerial office to proclaim the gospel and administer the sacraments in accordance with the gospel, so that in this way faith is awakened and strengthened'. For Lutherans the ecclesial office is a divine institution, although ordination is not usually characterized as a sacrament" (*Eucharist*, 67). But as ordination for both Catholics and Lutherans is done through the laying on of hands and the invocation of the Holy Spirit for his gifts for the proper exercise of ministry, this has led the dialogue commission to affirm that it sees more clearly than before that the question of whether ordination can be called a sacrament is chiefly a matter of terminology (cf. L–C *Malta*, 59; *Ways*, 69).[47]

> The Reformed-Catholic dialogue states, "Christ sends us into the world with the message of a new life and a new common life in fellowship with him. In our speaking and acting he bears witness to himself. His Gospel gathers, protects and maintains the koinonia of his disciples as a sign and beginning of his kingdom. He himself constantly calls this community to the

memorial of his death; he himself comes into its midst as the living One through his word and causes this word to take shape in the celebration of the Supper in which he deepens and seals (cf. *Jn* 15:4f, 6:56f, *1 Cor* 10:16) his fellowship with us and in which the new life of fellowship of Christendom is represented to the world (*1 Jn* 1:3). The presidence of the commissioned church office bearer at the celebration of the Meal effectively represents this unique role of Christ as the Lord and Host. The commissioned office-bearer is there to show the assembled community that it does not have disposal itself over the Eucharist but simply carries out obediently what Christ has commissioned the Church to do" (*Ref I*, 75).

On the question of ordination the Reformed–Catholic dialogue states, "The liturgical validation at the time of the act of ordination includes the invocation of the Holy Spirit (*'epiclesis'*) with the laying on of hands by other ordained ministers. The invocation of the Holy Spirit is a reminder of the essential role which the doctrine of the Trinity must fulfil in any balanced understanding of the ministry. It gives proper weight both to Jesus Christ's historical and present action and to the continual operation of the Holy Spirit. The laying on of hands is an efficacious sign which initiates and confirms the believer in the ministry conferred. It is not the community which produces and authorizes the office but the living Christ who bestows it on the community and incorporates this office into its life" (*Ref I*, 98). "Calvin himself did not object to calling ordination a Sacrament, but he did not count it on a level with baptism and Eucharist because it was not intended for all Christians (*Institutes* IV:19,28)" (*Ref II*, 140).

"For Methodists also the rule is that it is ordained ministers who preside at the eucharist. 'The eucharist, which sacramentally expresses the whole gospel, is the representative act of the whole Church, and it is fitting that the representative person should preside' " (M–C *Dublin,* 101 citing *Statement on Ordination*, British Methodist Conference, 1974).

f) *Issues for further study*

96. The Lutheran–Catholic dialogue reached a fundamental agreement on the real presence of the Lord in the Eucharist and on the sacrifice character of the Eucharist. But at the same time the dialogue raises questions which still need to be addressed and discussed by the other dialogues.

Still unresolved issues concern the doctrinal formulation and the duration of the eucharistic presence of the Lord. Lutherans do not use the term *transubstantiation*, but speak of a presence of Christ's body and blood in, with, and under bread and wine; this they see as a real analogy to the Lord's incarnation. The term *transubstantiation* is widely considered by them to be a rationalistic attempt to explain the eucharistic mystery, which can imply an overly naturalistic understanding. However, according to their Confessional writings they too can speak of a "change" (cf. Apol. X,2). When Catholics express this "change" by the term *transubstantiation* they are intending to preserve the character of the mystery, not to give an explanation of how the change occurs (cf. L–C *Eucharist*, 49-51).

With regard to the duration of the eucharistic presence Lutherans and Catholics agree that the eucharistic presence is directed toward believing reception, but that it is nevertheless not confined only to the moment of reception, nor does it depend on the faith of the receiver, however closely related to this it may be. "According to Catholic doctrine the Lord grants His presence even beyond the sacramental celebration for as long as the species of bread and wine remain. The faithful are accordingly invited to 'give to this holy sacrament in veneration the worship of latria, which is due to the true God' (citing the Council of Trent, DS 1643). Lutherans have not infrequently taken exception to certain of the forms of eucharistic piety connected with this conviction. They are regarded as inadmissibly separated from the eucharistic meal. On the other hand, Catholic sensibilities are offended by the casual way in which the elements remaining after communion are treated sometimes on the Lutheran side, and this indicates a discrepancy which is not yet overcome" (L–C *Eucharist,* 53–54).

In addition, the doctrine of the sacrificial character of the Eucharist still gives rise to disagreement. According to Catholic doctrine the sacrifice of the Mass is the making present of the sacrifice of the cross; it is not a repetition of this sacrifice and adds nothing to its saving significance. When thus understood, the sacrifice of the Mass is an affirmation and not a questioning of the uniqueness and full value of Christ's sacrifice on the cross. Nevertheless, Lutherans have feared that the understanding of the Eucharist as propitiatory sacrifice in contrary to the uniqueness and complete sufficiency of the sacrifice of the cross, so that even today the Lutheran tradition avoids any mention of the 'sacrifice of the Mass'. On the other hand the Lutheran Reformation affirmed the understanding of the Lord's Supper as a sacrifice of thanksgiving (cf. L–C *Eucharist,* 59-60).

The Reformed–Catholic dialogue states, "While we are aware of the serious discrepancy between our claims to common theological understanding and our actual practices.... We believe we have reached a common understanding of the meaning and purpose and basic doctrine of the Eucharist, which is in agreement with the Word of God and the universal tradition of the Church. We also believe that the way is clearly opening out before us on which remaining misunderstandings and disagreements about the Lord's Supper can be cleared up. The terminology which arose in an earlier polemical context is not adequate for taking account of the extent of common theological understanding which exists in our respective churches" (*Ref I*, 91; cf. *Ref II*, 152). Nonetheless the dialogue has convinced the partners of the urgent need to pursue the following questions: "the constitutive elements of a eucharistic service, especially in view of its relation to certain forms of Christian fellowship, called in some countries 'agape-celebrations'; the use of the Eucharist today which grows out of a faithful reflection on the tradition and on the vast changes which typify life today; the urgent contemporary pastoral questions of mutual eucharistic hospitality" (*Ref I*, 92).

The Methodist-Catholic dialogue identifies several areas where further dialogue is needed regarding the Eucharist. "The chief point of difference concerns the question of the transformation of the bread and wine into the body and blood of Christ. Roman Catholics affirm that the physical and chemical composition of the bread and wine remain un-changed, but that their inner reality is that of the body and blood of Christ. Methodists could use such expressions from the Windsor Statement as 'mysterious and radical change... in the inner reality of the elements' or 'become his body and blood' only in the sense that the bread and wine acquire an additional significance as effectual signs of the body and blood of Christ. They do not, however, consider this change to be of such a nature that the bread and wine cease to be bread and wine" (M–C *Dublin*, 59, citing ARCIC, *Eucharist*, 6; cf. M–C *Denver* 84).

"The Roman Catholic practice of reservation has the bringing of communion to the sick as its primary and original purpose. Adoration of Christ present in the elements is a secondary end. Both ends have their foundation in belief in the real presence. Methodists do not reserve the elements but reverently dispose of them" (M–C *Dublin*, 61). Roman Catholics "see the eucharist not as another sacrifice adding something to Christ's once-for-all sacrifice, nor as a repetition of it, but as making present in a sacramental way the same sacrifice. For some Methodists such language would imply that Christ is still being sacrificed. Methodists prefer to say that Christ has offered one sacrifice for sins and now lives to make intercession for us, so that we in union with him can offer ourselves to the Father, making his sacrificial death our only plea" (M–C *Dublin*, 66).

"In Methodism any Christian who can conscientiously accept the invitation is welcomed to the Lord's table. Except in cases of urgent necessity, eucharistic communion is extended by Roman Catholics only to those who share the same faith" (M–C *Denver*, 84). While for Methodists, "the rule is that it is ordained ministers who preside at the eucharist ... this does not imply that a eucharist is not valid unless an ordained minister presides, and the rule is therefore held to admit exceptions, when the conference recognizes a situation in which members of the church are in danger of being deprived of the eucharist, because there are no ordained ministers in their neighbourhood, and consequently grants a dispensation to a layman (in a particular area for a definite period of time) to preside at the eucharist. This is of rare occurrence, and it is a practice which is constantly under review" (M–C *Dublin*, 101).

More recently, the Seoul Report summarized remaining issues which would need to be resolved before Catholics and

Methodists could give full mutual recognition to each other's celebration of the Eucharist. "These include the nature and validity of the ministry of those who preside at the Eucharist, the precise meaning of the Eucharist as the sacramental 'memorial' of Christ's saving death and resurrection, the particular way in which Christ is present in Holy Communion, and the link between eucharistic communion and ecclesial communion. It is essential that these issues be further explored" (M–C *Seoul*, 94).

D.   REFLECTIONS ON CHAPTER FOUR

97.   Chapter Four shows that considerable consensus on baptism and a growing consensus on the Eucharist are emerging. Among the positive successes of the dialogues is the way that each of them has reflected on the centrality of the liturgy for the life of the Church. The old stereotype that the Catholic Church is the 'Church of the sacraments' as opposed to the Protestant communities as 'Churches of the Word' has been overcome. All parties are convinced about the intimate relation between Word and Sacrament.

One of the most significant areas of consensus is the common acknowledgment of each other's baptism. Through our common baptism we live already today in a real – albeit not full – ecclesial communion as our common baptism is the basis of the growing communion between us.

On the Eucharist, the ARCIC dialogue has achieved "substantial agreement" on essential points of eucharistic doctrine, especially on the Eucharistic presence and the sacrificial/memorial character of the Mass. Likewise, in the Catholic–Lutheran dialogues it is possible to speak of a high degree of agreement on both doctrines, although this has received no official recognition, and many issues remain unresolved.

A common theme in all the dialogues is the central role of Eucharist in giving life to, maintaining, expressing and deepening the *koinonia* of the Church. All the dialogues demonstrate a convergence in the common reflection on the biblical meaning of *anamnesis/memoria,* which helps to move beyond the old polemics about the Mass as sacrifice. Moreover, since the Second Vatican Council the importance of the *epiclesis,* and through this the role of the Holy Spirit in the Eucharist, was re–emphasized in the Catholic Church and among our dialogue partners. The issue of communion under both species is no longer a problem of principle since the reforms of Vatican II.

98. Alongside these precious and important achievements, the dialogues still reveal issues demanding further theological work. The consensus achieved on the sacrament of baptism may offer the possibility of reaching agreement on the fact that sacramental initiation involves baptism, confirmation and Eucharist. However, an area of concern relating to baptism is the extent to which previously agreed statements and principles are maintained in the practice of the dialogue partners. Some partners, despite agreement that baptism with water and biblical Trinitarian formula are essential, no longer see this as essential and increasingly employ non-traditional Trinitarian formulae. This is a real concern for the Catholic Church, requiring new clarifications and a new consensus, since the Catholic Church does not recognize baptism with a non–biblical Trinitarian formula (cf. Mt 28:19).

With regard to the sacrament of the Eucharist further clarifications are needed on the sacrificial character of the Mass, on the nature of the change wrought in the bread and wine, and on the real presence of our Lord in the Eucharist. Specifically, is Luther's own position on real presence as it is affirmed in the dialogues reconcilable with the Lutheran churches' widely accepted position of the Leuenberg Concord, and have the Lutheran-Reformed controversies about the real presence been overcome? What is the Protestant view of the permanent presence after the Eucharistic celebration? Can consensus be found about the meaning of the term *transubstantiation* repudiated by all the Reformers, or does the rejection of this term demonstrate that a deeper difference still remains in the understanding of the real presence of the Lord? Does the difference on the permanent presence of the Lord in the Eucharist point also to a deeper difference? More recently there have also been concerns about certain forms of Christian fellowship, called in some countries 'agape–celebrations'.

Questions can also be raised on the subject of eucharistic ministry, and in particular, whether there is consistency about the necessity for the minister of the Eucharist to be ordained. For Catholics it is a matter of concern that, contrary to what is stated and agreed in the dialogues, in many church communities non–ordained persons are permitted to preside at the Eucharistic celebration.

The question of eucharistic hospitality has arisen in some of the dialogues, doubtless in response to serious pastoral concerns. However, Catholic reluctance on this matter itself expresses concerns about a common doctrinal understanding of the eucharist as sacrament of faith, and about the inner connection between eucharistic communion and ecclesial communion (cf. L–C *Eucharist*, 72 f). Only when solid agreement on these unresolved questions is achieved will the issues of eucharistic hospitality and eucharistic sharing be capable of solution; this may indeed be an incentive to continue and intensify our dialogues.

In the light of these reflections, a further reading of the previous chapter on the Church reveals a growing ease with talking about the Church in a sacramental way, which could provide a context in which renewed discussion about other sacraments might be possible. It is appropriate to ask whether the scholastic distinction between *sacramenta maiora* and *sacramenta minora* is helpful for further dialogue on sacraments in general. Can the liturgical signs which Catholics call sacraments be seen by others as instruments of grace and new life in Jesus Christ? Often the dialogues use sacramental terminology without necessarily defining the term 'sacrament'; further discussion would be helpful in clarifying terminology and theology. This reintroduces the pivotal question on the sacramental character of the Church, and its concrete meaning and consequences.

Notes

38 Some Lutherans also call confession (penance) a sacrament on the basis of CA XII and Apol. XI-XII. Reflection on the sacramental character of other rites has also been part of the Methodist–Catholic dialogue (cf. M–C *Seoul,* 123). In this document, however, we concentrate on the two sacraments acknowledged by all four dialogue partners; both are also for Catholics the major sacraments.

39 Some Reformed communions have either removed or footnoted this statement in the Heidelberg Catechism to indicate that Question 80 does not accurately reflect the official teaching and practice of the contemporary Roman Catholic Church and is therefore no longer confessionally binding.

40 Early contributions were made by the Groupe des Dombes, *Pour la communion des Églises* (1988). The most important multilateral ecumenical text is the Lima document *Baptism, Eucharist and Ministry* (1982). The problem was taken up in

the German document *The Condemnations of the Reformation Era: Do They Still Divide?* (1994).

41 In the US Lutheran–Catholic dialogue the problem was dealt with at an early stage in *One Baptism for the Remission of Sins* (Lutherans and Catholics in Dialogue II, Augsburg/Minnesota 1966).

42 ARCIC's work on the Eucharist, contained in the 1971 agreed statement *Eucharistic Doctrine* and the 1979 *Eucharistic Doctrine: Elucidation,* was part of ARCIC I's *Final Report* which was submitted for an authoritative response from the Catholic Church and the Anglican Communion. On the official Anglican and Roman Catholic responses, and the ensuing *Clarifications*, see footnote 25. This official response process allows us to see in ARCIC's *Final Report* a consensus on basic truths pertaining to the nature of the Eucharist. ARCIC added two qualifiers: the Commission expressed its conviction "that if there are any remaining points of disagreement they can be resolved on the principles here established" (ARCIC *Eucharist,* 12); and that "differences of theology and practice may well coexist with a real consensus on the essentials of eucharistic faith – as in fact they do within each of our communions" (*Eucharist Elucidation,* 9).

43 Responding to queries about the meaning of *memorial* in this context, ARCIC's *Eucharist Elucidation* notes that the notion of *anamnesis* "enables us to affirm a strong conviction of sacramental realism and to reject mere symbolism." Regarding sacrifice and memorial, the text proceeds to state: "[I]t is possible to say at the same time that there is only one unrepeatable sacrifice in the historical sense, but that the eucharist is a sacrifice in the sacramental sense, provided that it is clear that this is not a repetition of the historical sacrifice. There is therefore one historical, unrepeatable sacrifice, offered once for all by Christ and accepted once for all by the Father. In the celebration of the memorial, Christ in the Holy Spirit unites his people with himself in a sacramental way so that the Church enters into the movement of his self-offering" (*Eucharist Elucidation* 5; cf. *Clarifications*).

44 *Eucharist Elucidation* 6 added, "*Becoming* does not here imply material change. Nor does the liturgical use of the word imply that the bread and wine become Christ's body and blood in such a way that in the eucharistic celebration his presence is limited to the consecrated elements. It does not imply that Christ becomes present in the eucharist in the same manner that he was present in his earthly life. It does not imply that this *becoming* follows the physical laws of this world".

45 The US Lutheran–Catholic dialogue: *The Eucharist as Sacrifice* (Lutherans and Catholics in Dialogue III, Augsburg/Minnesota, 1967). The German dialogue deepened reflection on the problem: *Das Opfer Jesu Christi und seine Gegenwart in der Kirche: Klärungen zum Opfercharakter des Herrenmahls.* Hrsg. von K. Lehmann-E. Schlink (Dialog der Kirchen, 3), Freiburg i. Br./Göttingen 1983.

46 This problem was dealt with in the US Lutheran–Catholic dialogue *Eucharist and Ministry* (Lutherans and Catholics in Dialogue IV, Washington DC 1970).

47 Cf. footnote 27 on the question of *defectus ordinis*.

Some Preliminary Conclusions

99. After more than forty years of official ecumenical dialogue with the Anglican Communion, and the Lutheran, Reformed and Methodist churches it may be asked: Where are we? What has been achieved and what still has to be done? Where can we and where should we go forward? To what extent have the dialogues resolved the core issues over which Christians separated in the sixteenth century? And what are the unresolved questions that still need to be taken up in the next decade?

Having examined the bilateral dialogues at the international level, some preliminary conclusions can be formed. There are many positive results to be identified, but fundamental questions on which we still diverge must also be recognized.

A. A RICH HARVEST

100. In the first place, it can happily be stated that some of the classic disputes, which were at the root of our painful divisions, have today been basically resolved through a new consensus on fundamental points of doctrine. In other disputed questions there is at least convergence, which has helped the dialogues to move beyond previous polemical stances, and has created a more relaxed ecumenical atmo-

sphere in which an *'exchange of gifts'* has been enriching for both sides.

101. *Our shared apostolic faith.* In contrast with former polemics and apologetics, contemporary ecumenical dialogue starts with what we have in common, rather than what divides us. In common we share the Gospel as the Word of God and the Good News for all humanity, and we share the Creeds of the first centuries which summarise the Gospel message and give an authentic interpretation of it. We confess together the Triune God, and that Jesus Christ our common Lord and Saviour is truly human and truly divine, the one and universal mediator between God and man. Together we confess that there is one, holy, catholic and apostolic Church, to which in different ways we belong, so that even in our differences, we are brothers and sisters in the one Lord and in the one Spirit of Christ. Thus our dialogues can confirm and deepen our common foundation in the one apostolic faith and in our real but still incomplete communion.

102. *A fresh and renewed understanding of the relation between Scripture and Tradition.* Since the sixteenth century Christians have been divided not only on specific questions of faith, but have been also burdened by a conflict of approaches regarding how and with which criteria to resolve those questions. Can answers be found to our problems by appealing to Scripture alone (*sola scriptura*) or must argument derive from Scripture and Tradition? Today, it is no longer possible to set Scripture and Tradition at odds with each other, and such a sharp contrast is no longer tenable. Scripture itself is a product of the earliest Tradition and the later Tradition (in its theological sense) is to be understood as the living presence of the same Gospel throughout the ages right up to the present. In the Church, Tradition makes present and interprets the message

of the Bible in every age. It is wrong to make an abstraction from this interpretation; we cannot simply have immediate access to Scripture by jumping over two millennia and ignoring the intervening history of interpretation.

During this long history, the Christian community read and interpreted the Scriptures guided by the Holy Spirit. So it is that Catholics and other Christians are heirs to that rich history of two thousand years: the patristic and medieval tradition, the Reformation, the Catholic renewal in the sixteenth century, the post-Reformation developments, and the missionary and ecumenical movements. Still, we have learned to distinguish between the *Tradition* and the many *traditions* (mostly good and helpful, but sometimes also distorted and antithetical to the Gospel). Faced with such a complex history, we agree upon the primacy of Scripture within this historical interpretative process. For all of us, Scripture is the witness to the original and primeval normative apostolic Tradition, given once and for all times. Catholics and other Christians venerate the Scriptures as the inspired Word of God. To them we must listen with an open-minded, conversion-oriented, prayerful attitude, to understand what the Spirit is communicating through its words, stories, images, admonitions and wisdom – and through their interpretation in the course of history. The reception of such insights in both Catholic and other Christian communities has been a source of spiritual renewal and indeed has led to a high degree of shared biblical spirituality, and new awareness of our common mission to evangelisation.

103. *Basic agreement on the doctrine of justification.* The core message of the Bible is God's gracious and merciful salvific will to reconcile sinful humanity with himself, and to bring reconciliation and peace (*shalom*) to our divided and chaotic

world, where people are so often broken in themselves and alienated from one another. This is the meaning of the doctrine of justification. Previously, different and contradictory interpretations of justification weakened Christian witness to the world. With the *JDDJ* it was possible to see anew that the affirmation of *sola gratia* and *sola fide* does not contradict the affirmation that by grace we are made capable of bearing good fruits through works of justice, mercy and active love. It has become clear that through justification God's saving grace calls, frees and capacitates us for holiness and personal sanctification, as the starting point for the penetration of all worldly realities with the spirit of the Gospel. In this way it has proved possible to give common witness to the hope that is in us.

104. *Deepened understanding of the nature of the Church.* God does not call and justify us only as individuals; he calls, gathers and sanctifies us as his chosen people and royal priesthood in order that we might give common witness to his marvellous deeds. So the nature and mission of the Church belong together; the Church is missionary by its very nature. In the past, the understanding of this reality of the Church was divided by the sharply contrasting visions of a visible institutional Church and a hidden, spiritual Church; a Church as *mater et magistra* and a Church under the Gospel; a Church as sacrament of grace and Church as *creatura verbi*. At the same time, many elements of convergence have been found in these and other controversies. The Trinitarian roots of the Church have been re-emphasized, and there has been a focus on its nature as *koinonia/communio*.

This has brought about a convergence in our understanding of ministries in the Church, and has even given rise to a new and important openness to reconsidering such a long disputed and controversial issue as the Petrine ministry. It is true that none of these issues has been resolved through a full or even only a partial consensus. Yet it must be acknowledged that the convergence already achieved has confirmed and deepened our real (if still incomplete) communion, and has created a new and positive climate of practical cooperation in many fields of private, ecclesial, cultural, social and political life.

105. *New approaches to the sacraments of baptism and Eucharist.* Through baptism, the sacrament of faith, we are reborn to new life in Christ and incorporated into the Church, the body of Christ. Because of our separation we have not always recognized each other's baptism, as cases of re-baptism indicate. The rediscovery of our common baptism has helped Catholics and other Christians to recognise each other again as brothers and sisters in Christ, which in turn has led to official inter-church recognition of each other's baptism. This shared understanding of baptism is formulated in numerous valuable ecumenical statements.

Furthermore, we have rediscovered the centrality of liturgy, especially the liturgy of the Eucharist as source and summit of the Church. It was precisely the sacrificial character of the Eucharist and the real and true presence of Christ that occasioned some of the most forceful controversies of the Reformation era. Through the biblical idea of *anamnesis/ memoria,* ecumenical dialogue has unveiled new perspectives of understanding. This has made possible convergences (in some dialogues substantial, even if not yet full) on these matters, although they still require further progress towards a basic common understanding. The same is true in the rediscovery of the importance of the *epiclesis,* and thereby of the Holy Spirit as the main agent in the liturgy of the Eucharist and of all sacraments. All this is the more important because it leads us to hope that in the future (whether near or remote is not ours to determine) we may together celebrate the Eucharist as the sign of full communion.

B.   Questions for Further Discussion

106. As a second point, it must be acknowledged honestly and realistically that although our dialogues have brought progress, they have not yet led us to the final goal of full visible communion. The churches find themselves at an intermediate stage, confronted by difficult fundamental questions to which they give conflicting answers. It is not the intention here to specify all the remaining differences; it is only possible to focus on some basic central questions that have emerged in the analysis of our dialogues as presented in this paper.

107. *A new Symbolic Theology.* Although official Church confessions and statements refer to the common apostolic faith as witnessed by Scripture and the early Creeds, in practice the churches display a wide spectrum of contrasting interpretations. At times there is even a rejection of what other churches hold as binding affirmations of basic common ground. In the early stages of dialogue important contributions to the search for agreement were offered by the theology of God's Word in the so–called dialectical theology, in the renewed Lutheran theology and in the follow–up to the Oxford movement. More recently, however, positions akin to the *History of Religions* school of thought have emerged, together with newer liberal, social, analytical or post-modern positions. As a result our dialogue partners sometimes find it difficult to formulate their own position, and what constitutes their binding and obligatory doctrine. A renewal of what J. A. Möhler, a

forerunner and inspirer of today's ecumenical theology, called Symbolic Theology *(Symbolik)* – that is, a theology based on the binding creeds or confessions – seems necessary.

108. *Fundamental hermeneutical problems.* Helpful and open-ended perspectives have emerged on the relationship between Scripture and Tradition. But questions remain: What does the primacy of Scripture within the Tradition actually mean? To what extent and in what sense are binding interpretations of Scripture contained in Tradition? Who ultimately decides about the binding interpretation of our common apostolic heritage? On the issue of the Magisterium there still exists a significant asymmetry, and the unresolved differences between the churches mean that we are often unable to speak with one voice. It is therefore important to discover the teaching authority as a gift, being a point of reference and an instrument of unity, while at the same time recognizing that it is situated within the dynamic life of the Church as a whole, whose faith is witnessed to by charisms, the liturgy and the *sensus fidelium.*

A further key question has arisen from the modern historical critical methods of biblical exegesis that have emerged since the Enlightenment. While not denying the good use which can be made of these methods and the positive results they have already achieved, on occasion their presumed results contradict our common inherited Tradition and are frequently in conflict among themselves. In such a pluralistic exegetical situation the Reformation axiom of *Scriptura sui ipsius interpres* (Scripture as its own interpreter) is no longer convincing for many. What the primacy of Scripture concretely means and how a binding interpretation of Scripture is possible are therefore urgent and fundamental hermeneutical questions that await resolution.

109. *Focus on anthropology.* The consensus on basic truths of the doctrine of justification is without doubt a milestone, and a permanent achievement of ecumenical dialogue. It is, however, a consensus only on *basic* truths. There still exist different positions in respect to other truths intimately related to those basic ones, which carry repercussions for the very meaning of the term *basic consensus.* Examples would be the questions of *simul iustus et peccator,* of human cooperation and of personal sanctification, (that is, the new life in Christ). These are questions which go beyond what has already been achieved and need further clarification.

At this point the crucial question of theological anthropology must be faced for this is at the root of Western church divisions and is one of the most urgent issues confronting society today. Differences that have recently emerged on ethical questions – such as marriage and family as the cradle of human society and school of its culture, or human sexuality – are a sign of this challenging situation. Just as challenging are the connected issues of social, political and environmental ethics, for as people reconciled with God we must be peacemakers and witnesses of reconciliation to the world. So the solution of these anthropological and ethical questions is a prerequisite if we are to realise our common mission in today's world.

110. *The sacramental nature of the Church.* The main question which still divides the churches is the understanding of the Church itself. Significant progress has been made towards a shared understanding of the Church as communion and the ministries which, through Word and sacraments, are instruments of communion. However, the question of where the Church of Christ is to be concretely found and encountered, and in her full sense exists (that is, where she subsists) has

today become a central question – often cast in strong and polemical terms. Recent disputes on this issue are in danger of obscuring the many previous positive results of the dialogues.

Oversimplifying, it might be said that different ways of understanding the Church are frequently discussed. According to the Catholic *sacramental* view, the Church of Christ and her whole mystery, without overlooking its charismatic dimension, subsists in a concrete and permanent institutional structure, in communion with the bishop of Rome and the bishops in communion with him. The other view, without totally abandoning the institutional aspect, holds an understanding of the Church as *event*, existing wherever the Gospel is correctly preached and the sacraments duly administered. Another contrast often made is between privileging the local worshipping congregation as church in the primary sense, and taking the Church as the communion of local congregations/ churches made one by the communion between their chief pastors in the episcopal *ordo* of which the principle and foundation of unity is given personally as the Bishop of Rome. In the coming years the dialogues should focus on these questions and strive to see these views as complementary rather than as contradictory in a sacramental ecclesiological perspective.

This last point returns to the fundamental and all-determining question regarding the sacramental nature of the Church, and the relationship between God's sovereign action and the human and ecclesial cooperation that is thereby made possible. To formulate it in another way: in considering the relationship between Jesus Christ and the Church, the fundamental question arises of the relationship of *solus Christus* to the Augustinian *totus Christus, caput et membra* (Christ as head of the Church in relation to the members of the Church as His body). These are basic issues which need further discussion and investigation. The remaining unresolved questions regarding church ministries can then be treated in this wider and more promising context.

This is all the more important as these current fundamental differences give rise to conflicting theories on what full church communion means, and therefore what the very goal of the ecumenical movement should be, and where we should be moving ahead. While there can be several intermediate steps on the level of spiritual and practical ecumenism,[48] the ultimate goal is neither unity on the basis of the lowest common denominator, nor peaceful coexistence, nor uniformity, but visible full communion in faith, sacramental life, apostolic ministry and mission according to the image of the unity of Father, Son and Holy Spirit within the Holy Trinity.

111. *Eucharist — sacrament of unity.* Ecclesiological issues as yet unresolved, and the divergent answers given to them, have consequences for the question of our shared understanding of the common celebration of, and full participation in, the Eucharist as sign and instrument of full ecclesial communion. This is a pressing matter, also from the pastoral point of view.

If we are to reach the point of a common sharing at the Lord's table, our dialogues will once more have to address the themes of the real presence and the sacrificial character of the Eucharist understood as *anamnesis*. Much has already been done; but there still remain serious differences on the real and true presence of the Lord 'in and under' the species of bread and wine. On the sacrificial character of the Eucharist important theological convergences have emerged, but not yet a reception on the part of the churches, apart from ARCIC. Specifically, more clarification is required as to how, and in what sense, the Eucharist is the *memorial representation* of the one and unique sacrifice of Christ on the cross, through the Church's Eucharistic celebration understood as sacrifice. Finally, a solution is required to the remaining questions on the ministry in the Church, which as ministry of unity is also ministry of the Eucharist as sacrament of Church unity.

C.   An Outlook of Hope

112. The unanswered questions may cast a shadow over the rich results of more than forty years of dialogue. But it does not help to ignore or obscure unresolved problems; the first step towards solving problems is to identify them. What we have achieved with God's help offers hope for further positive steps on our ecumenical pilgrimage.

It must be acknowledged that our ecumenical dialogues cannot of themselves realise the final goal and ultimate hope of the ecumenical movement; that movement is an impulse and work of the Holy Spirit. The process of ecumenical reconciliation and rapprochement is therefore primarily a spiritual process, inspired by the hope that results from the belief that for God nothing is impossible (*Lk 1.37; Mk 10,27*).

It is with this hope that this 'Harvest Project' is presented to our Church and our ecumenical partners, for further study and discussion. It is our desire that it may initiate a process of reception of what we have achieved, and may promote further dialogues on remaining questions.

The dialogues undertaken so far show that they can pave the way for that which is the will of the Lord and the deep longing of so many Christians: that all be one in sharing the one table of the Lord. In this way our ecumenical dialogues, enriched by what we have achieved with God's help in past decades, will embark upon a new — and hopefully equally fruitful — stage, perhaps less enthusiastic and more sober, but nonetheless full of hope and filled with the *'dynamis'* of the Spirit.

NOTES

48 See, for example, Cardinal Kasper's *A Handbook of Spiritual Ecumenism*.